THIS COLORING BOOK BELONGS TO:

Color Chart

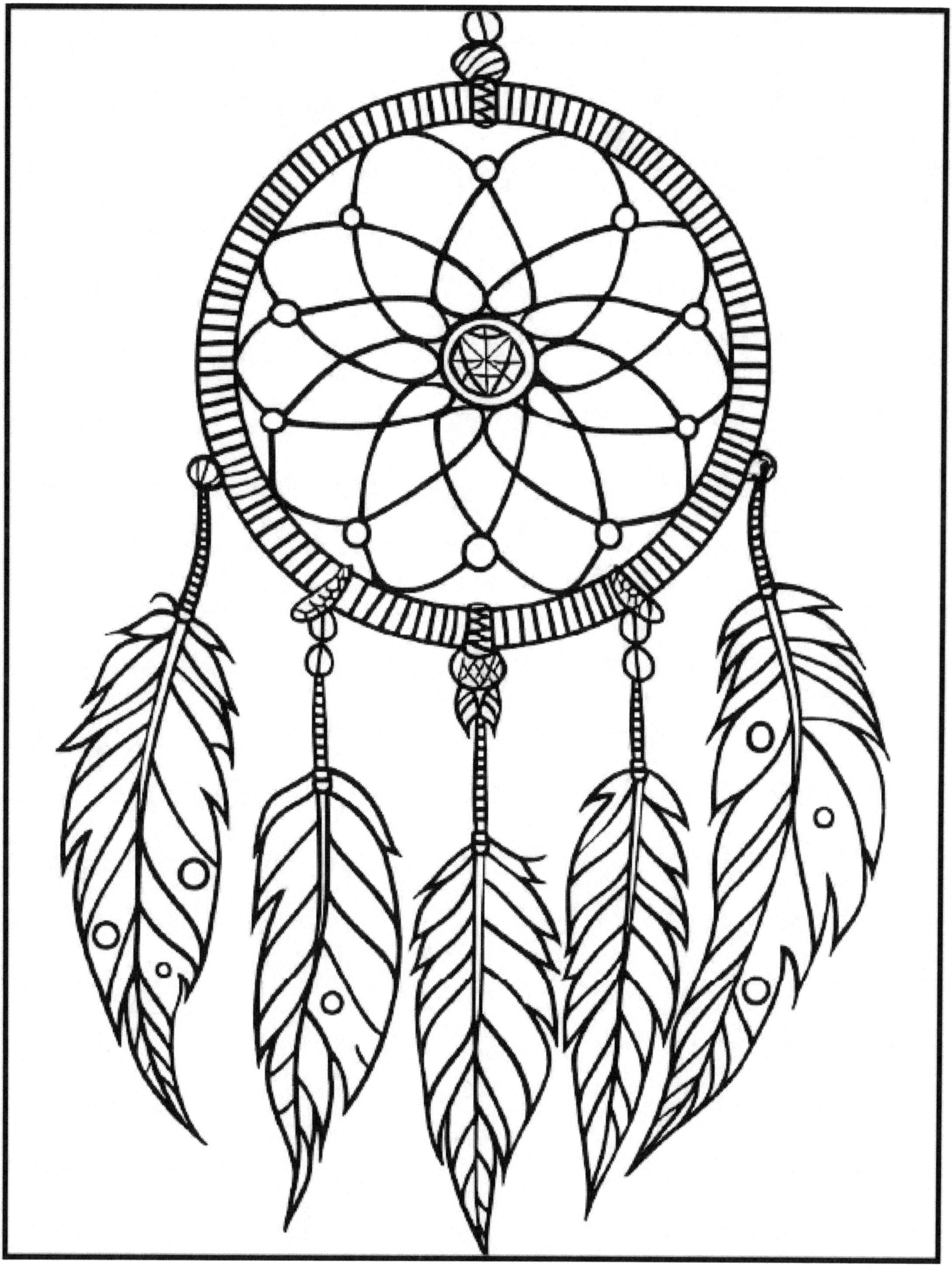

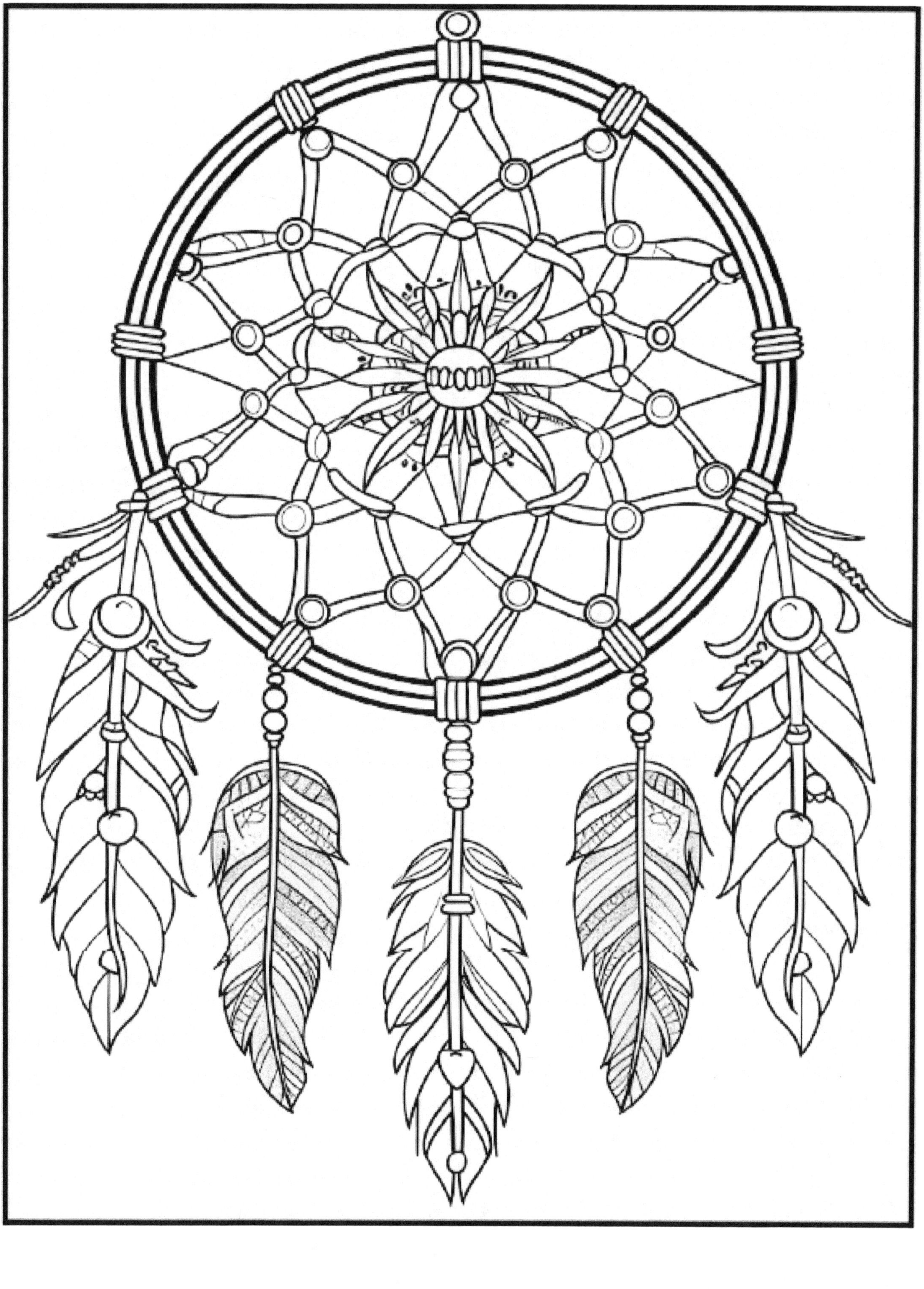

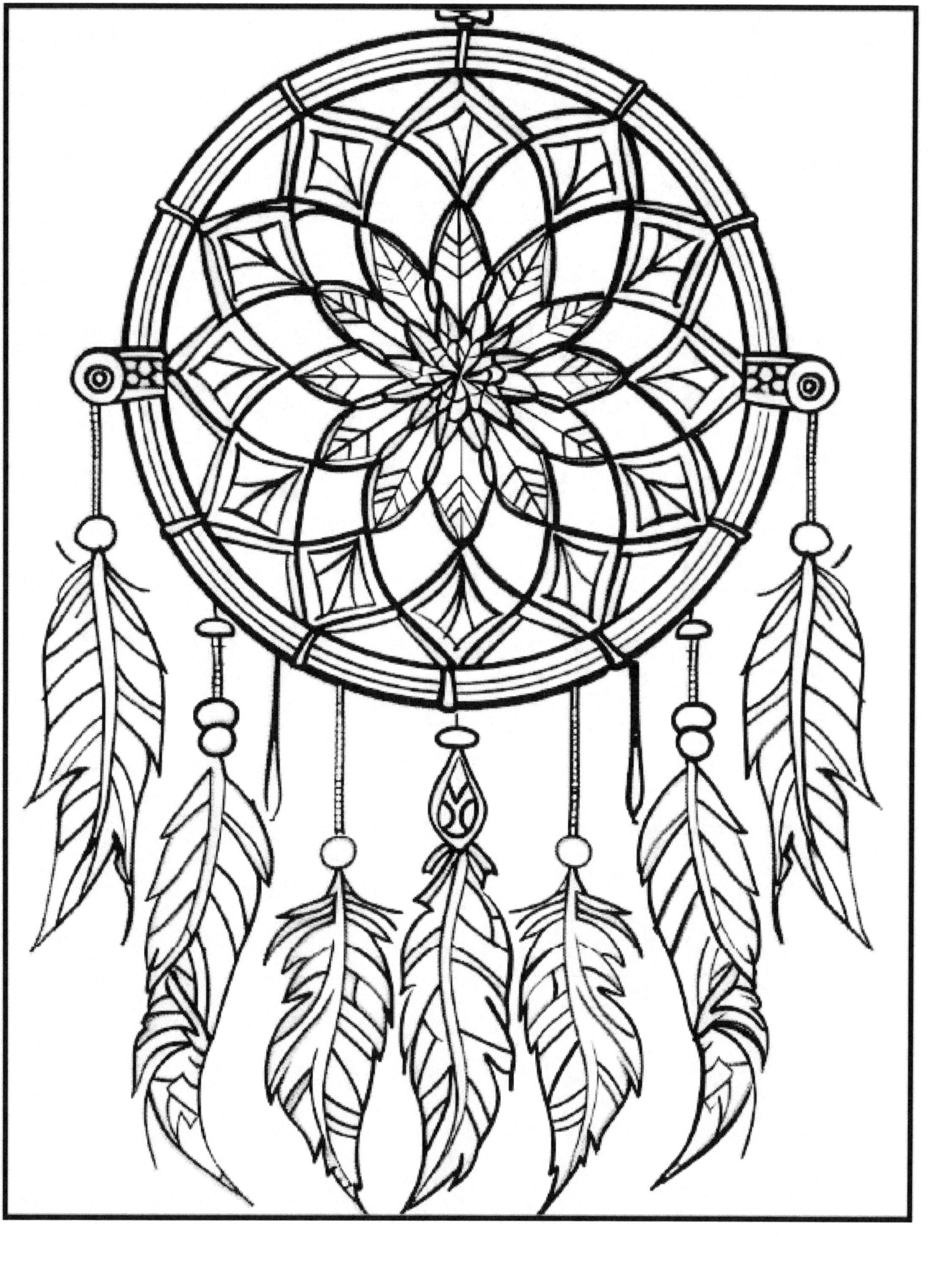

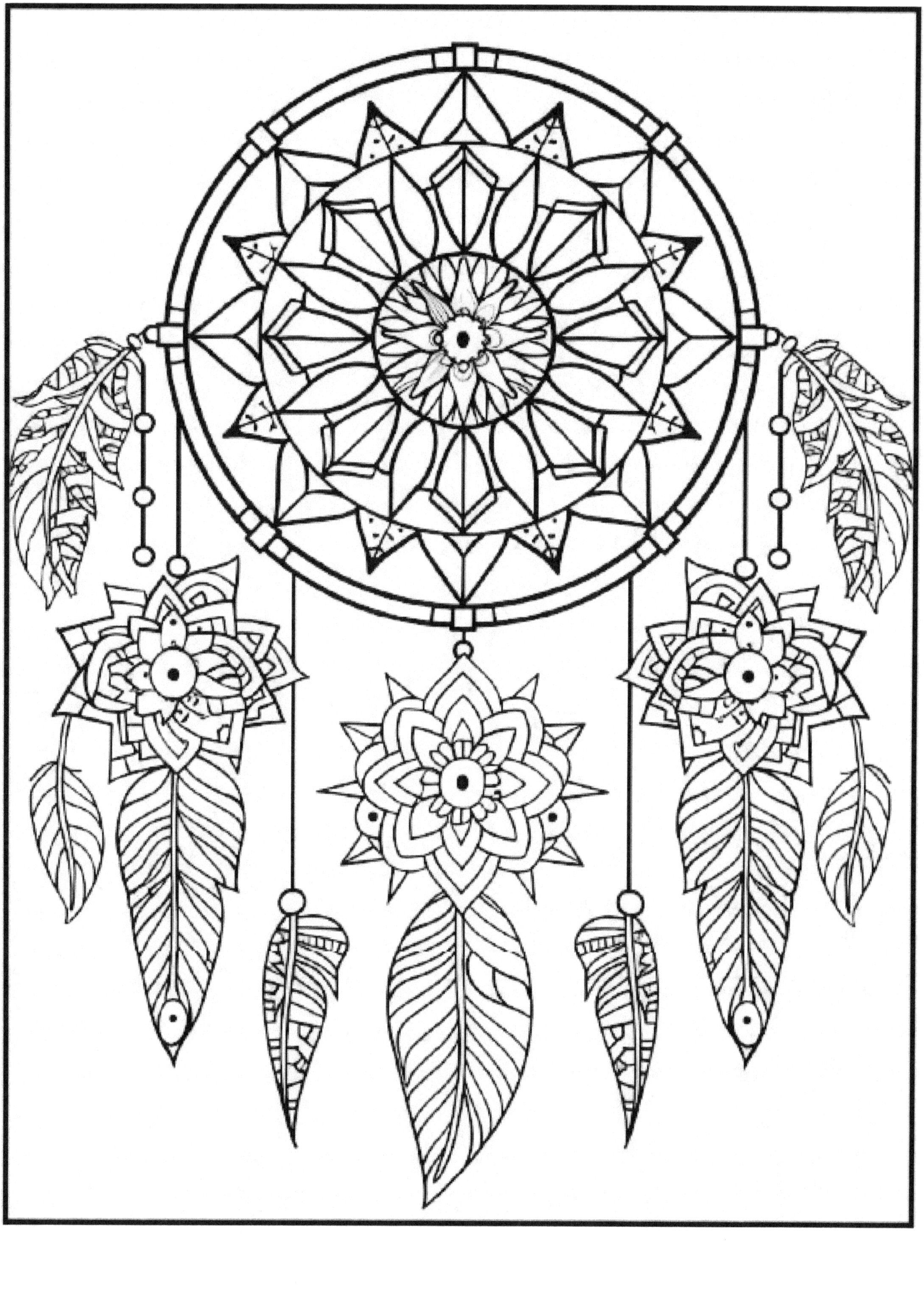

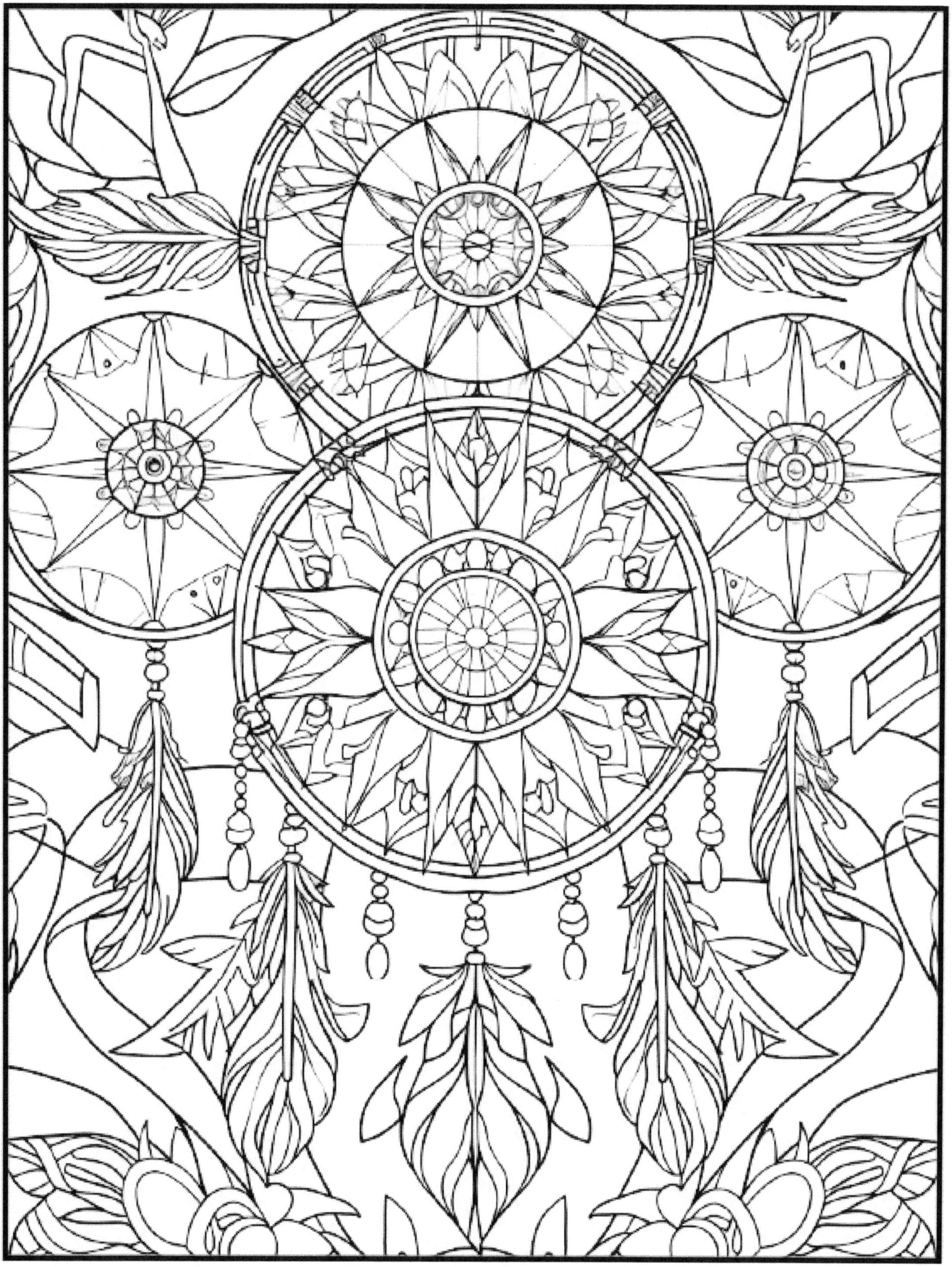

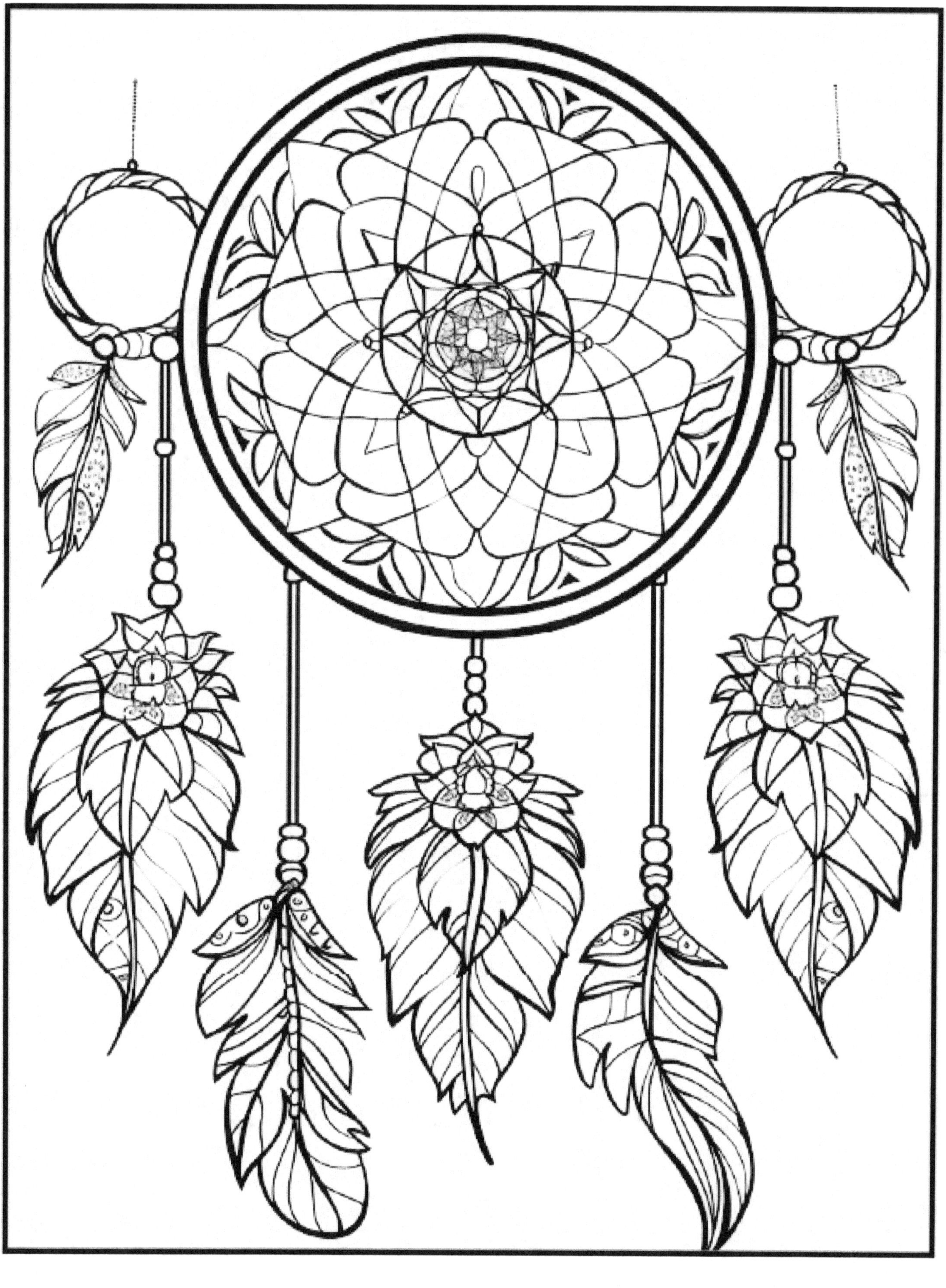

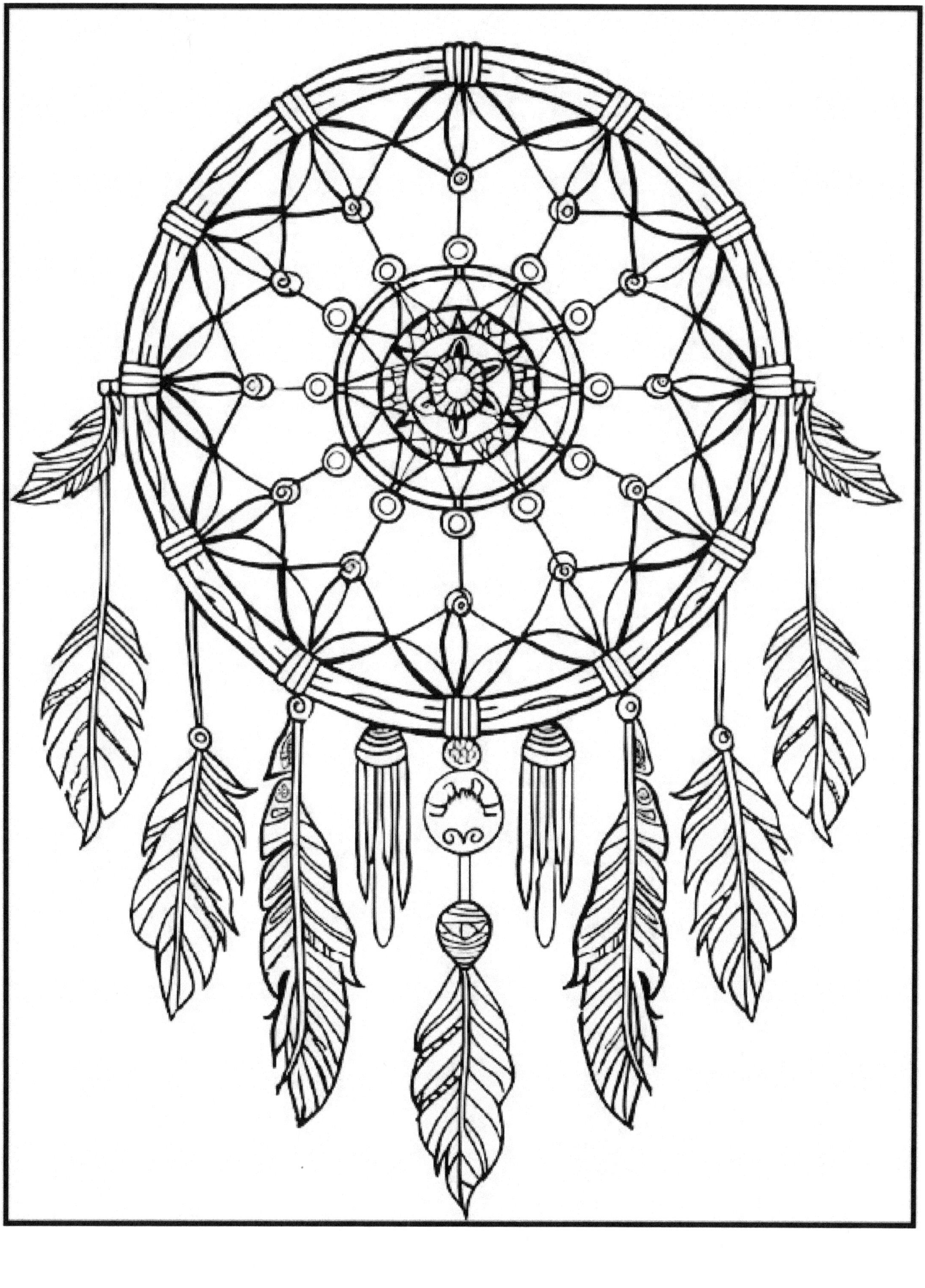

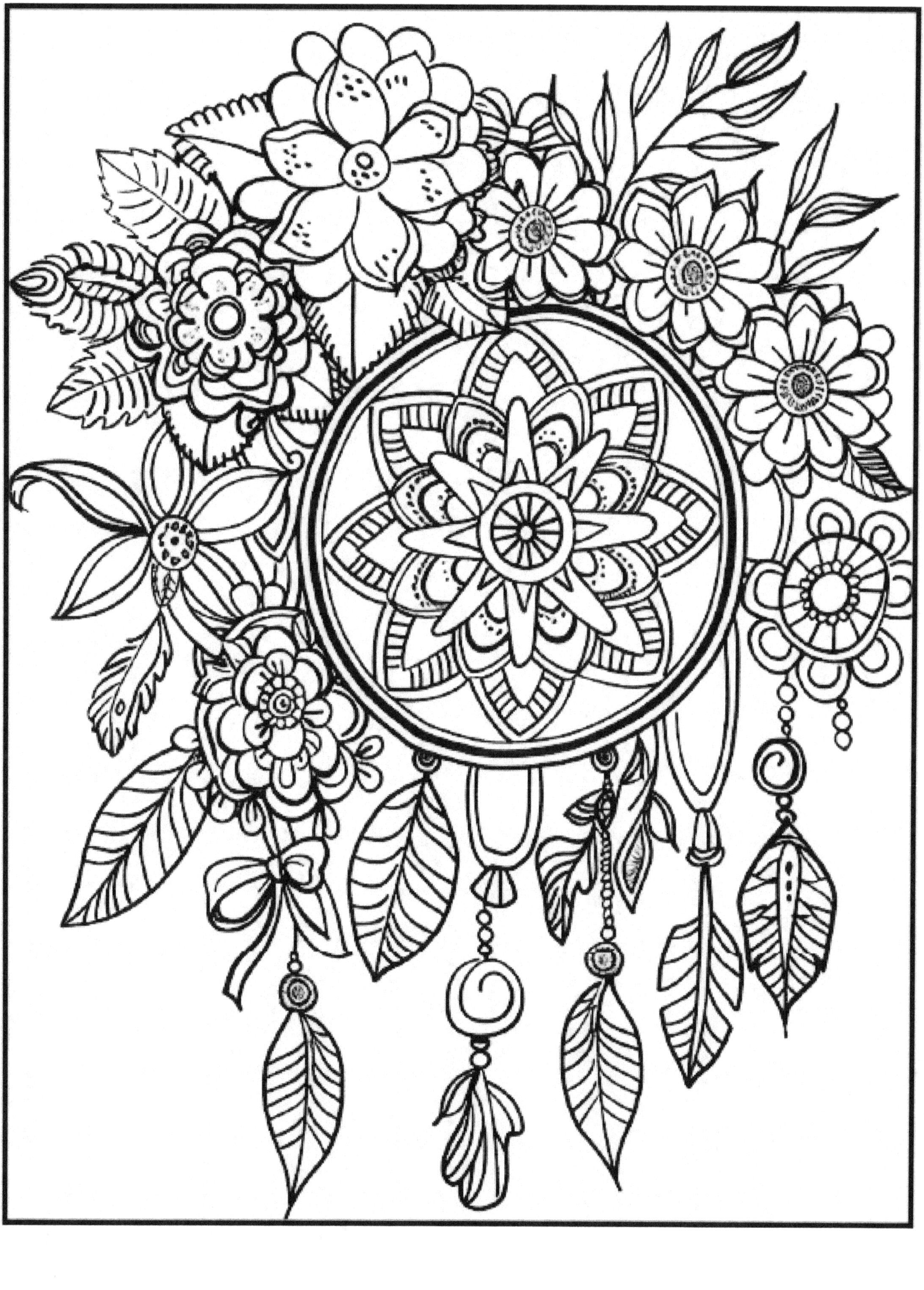

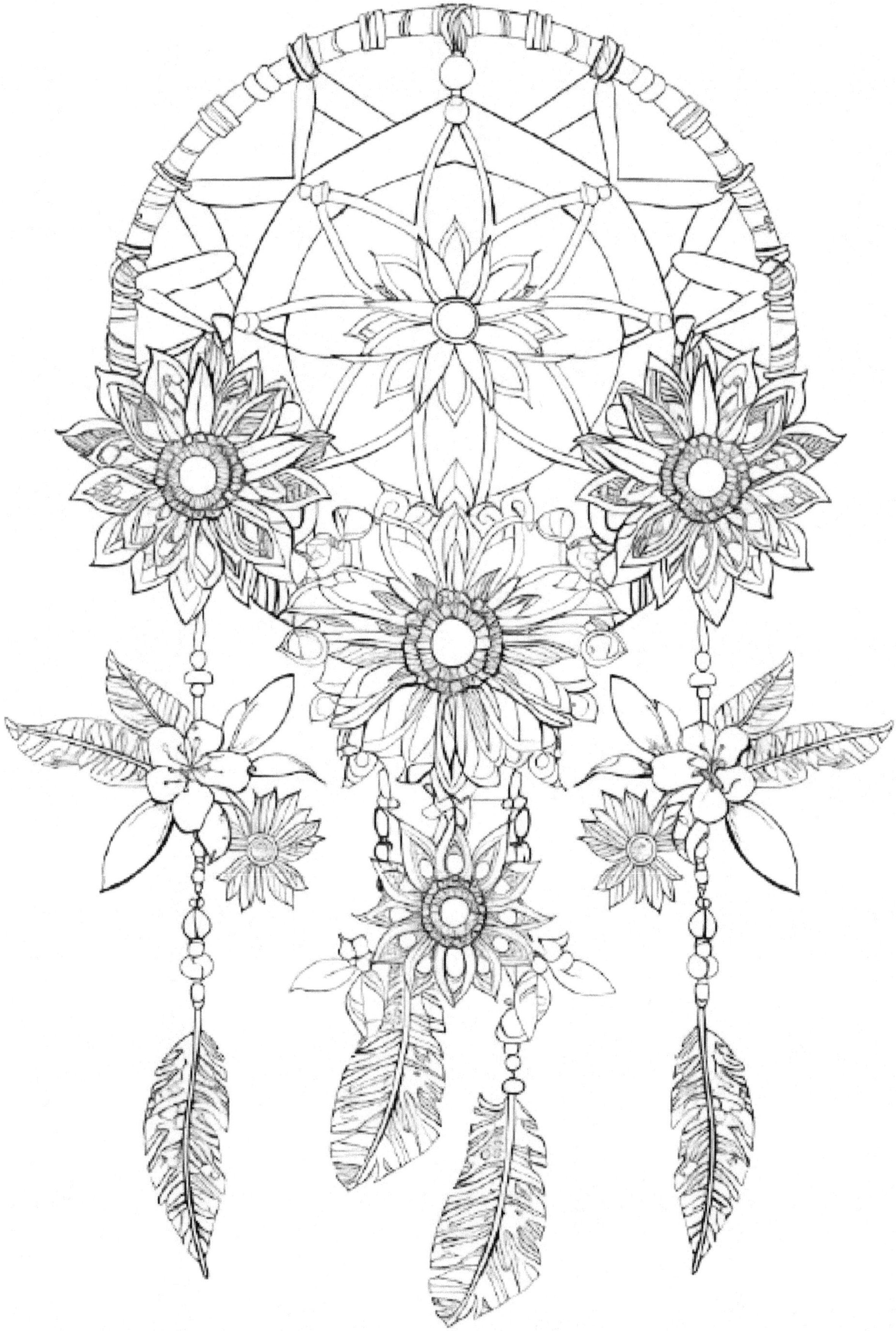

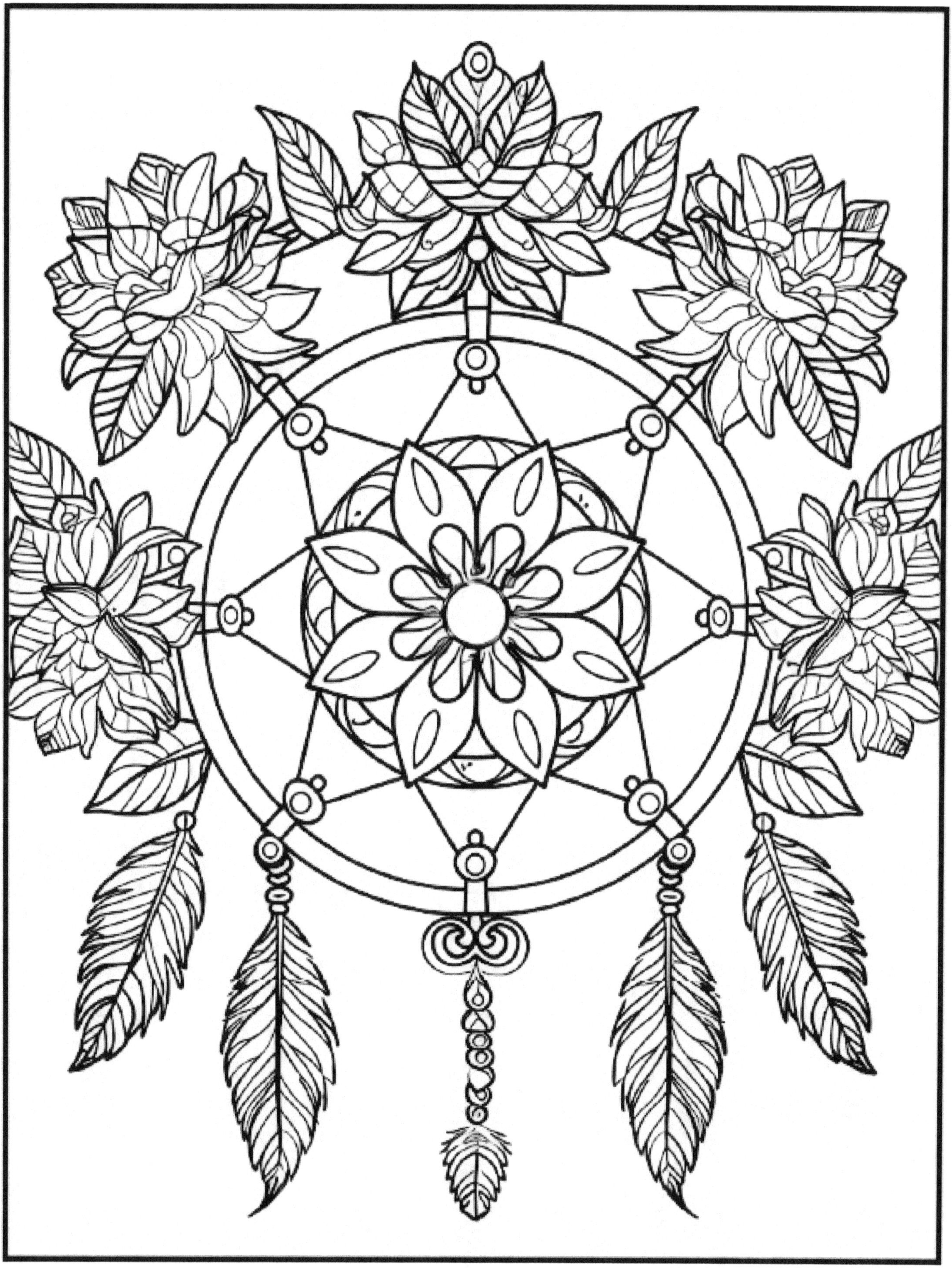

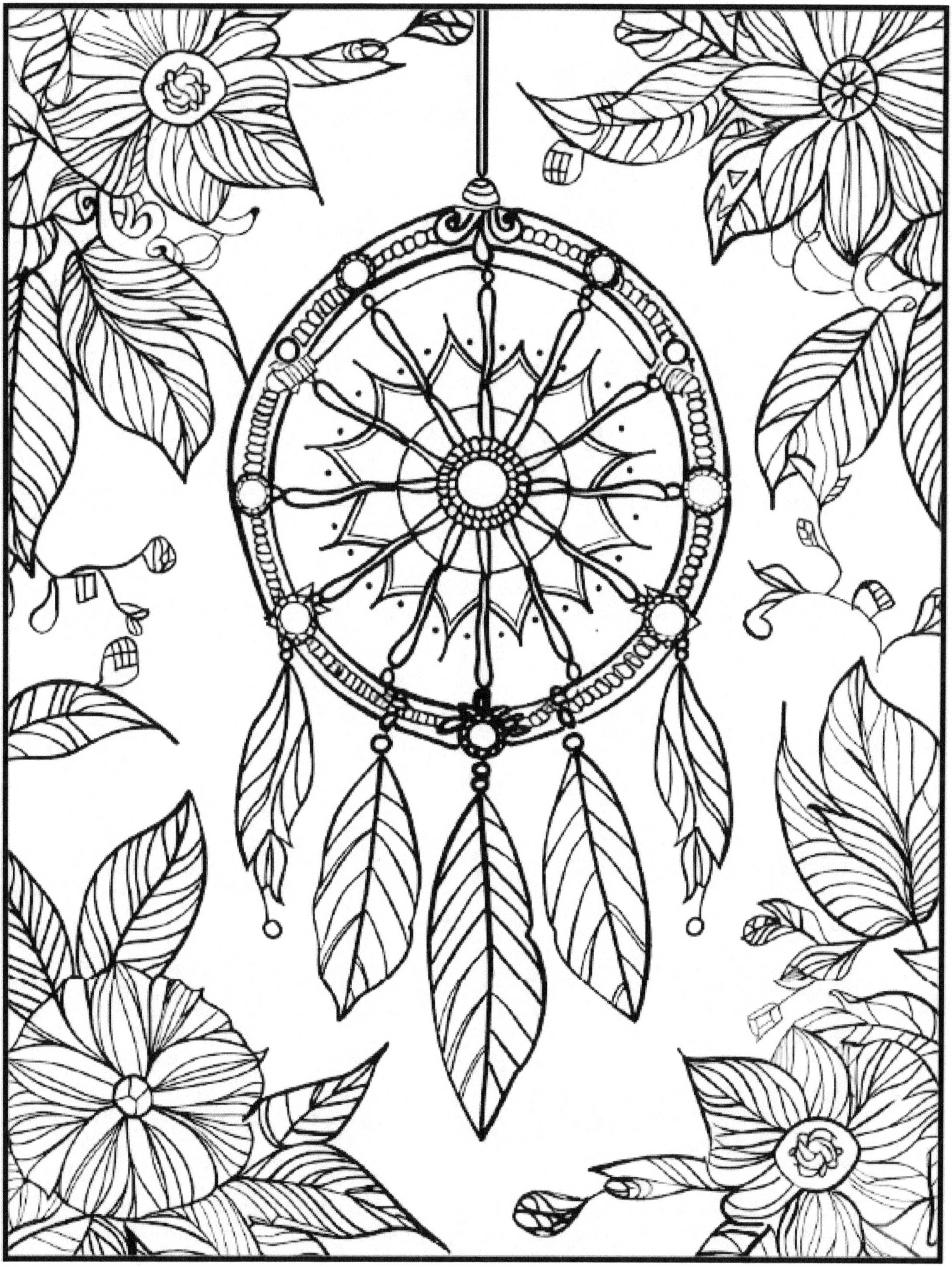

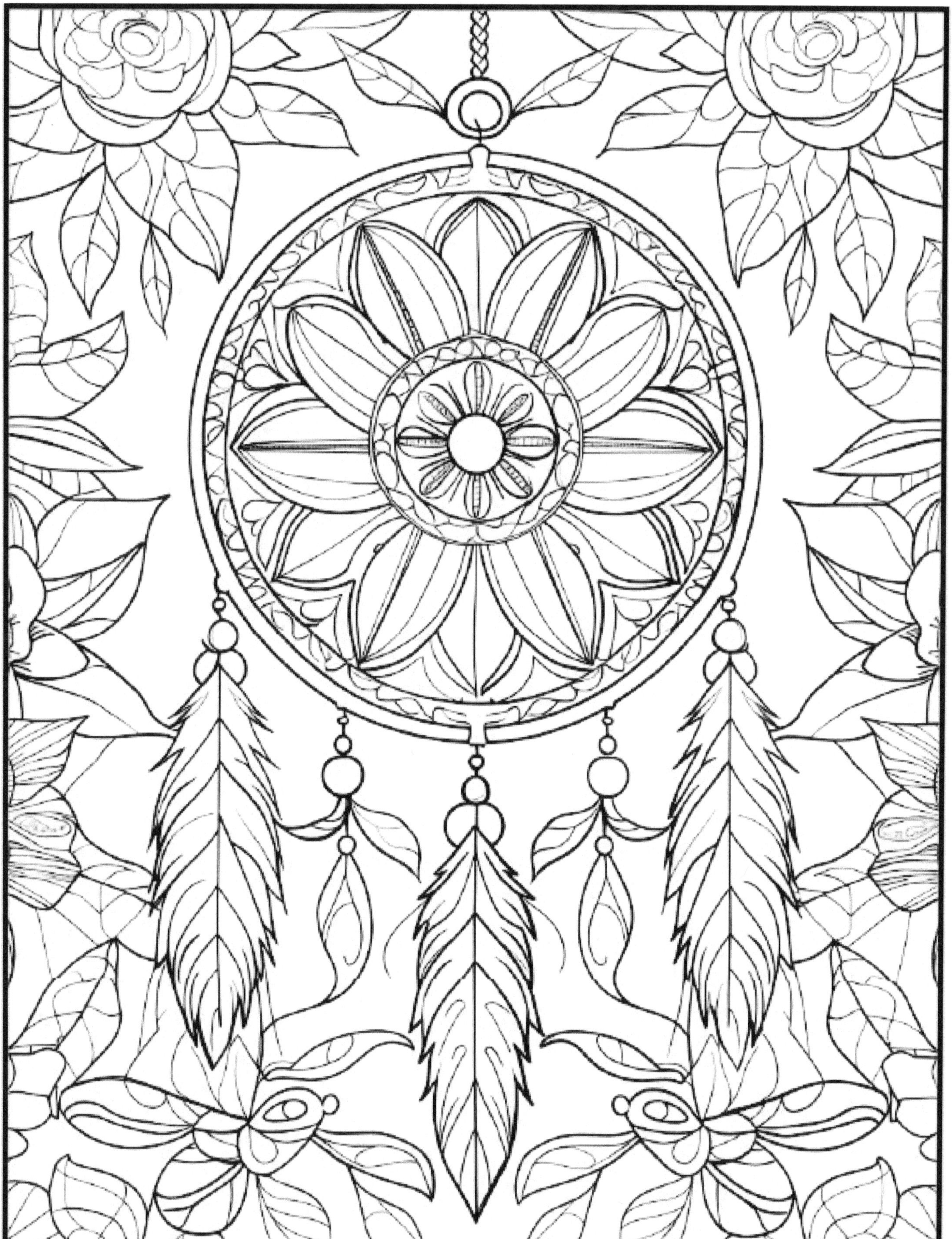

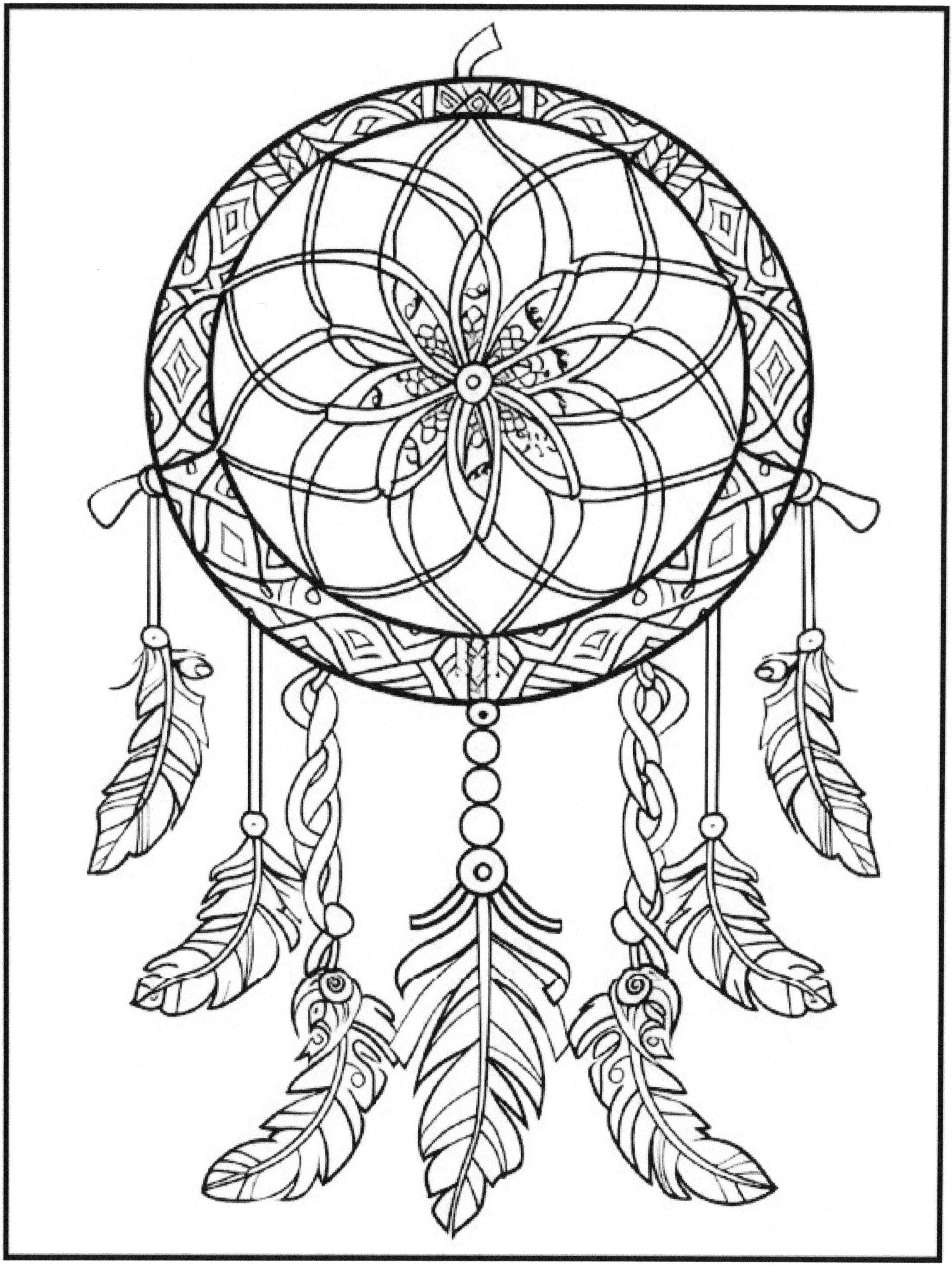

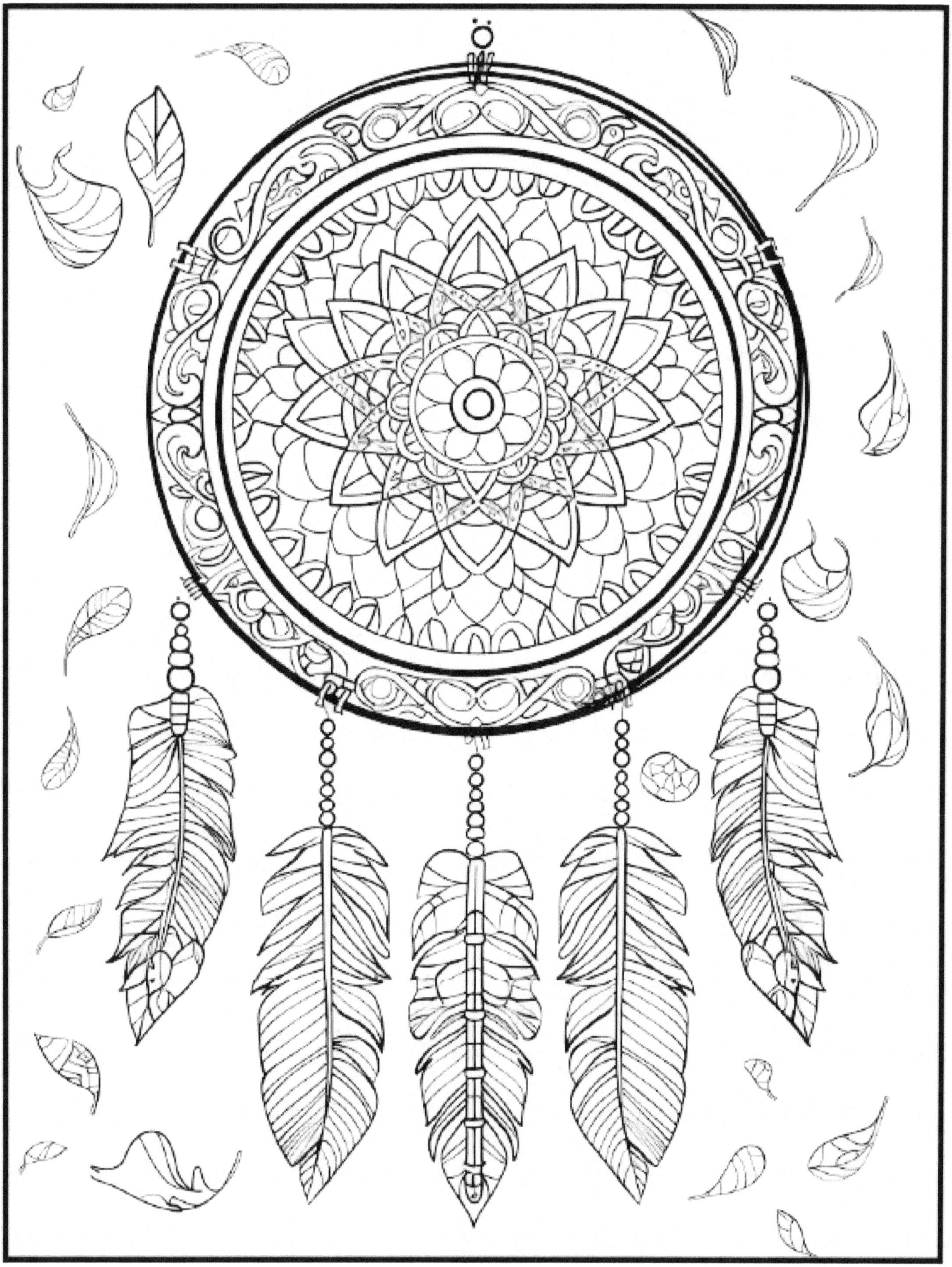

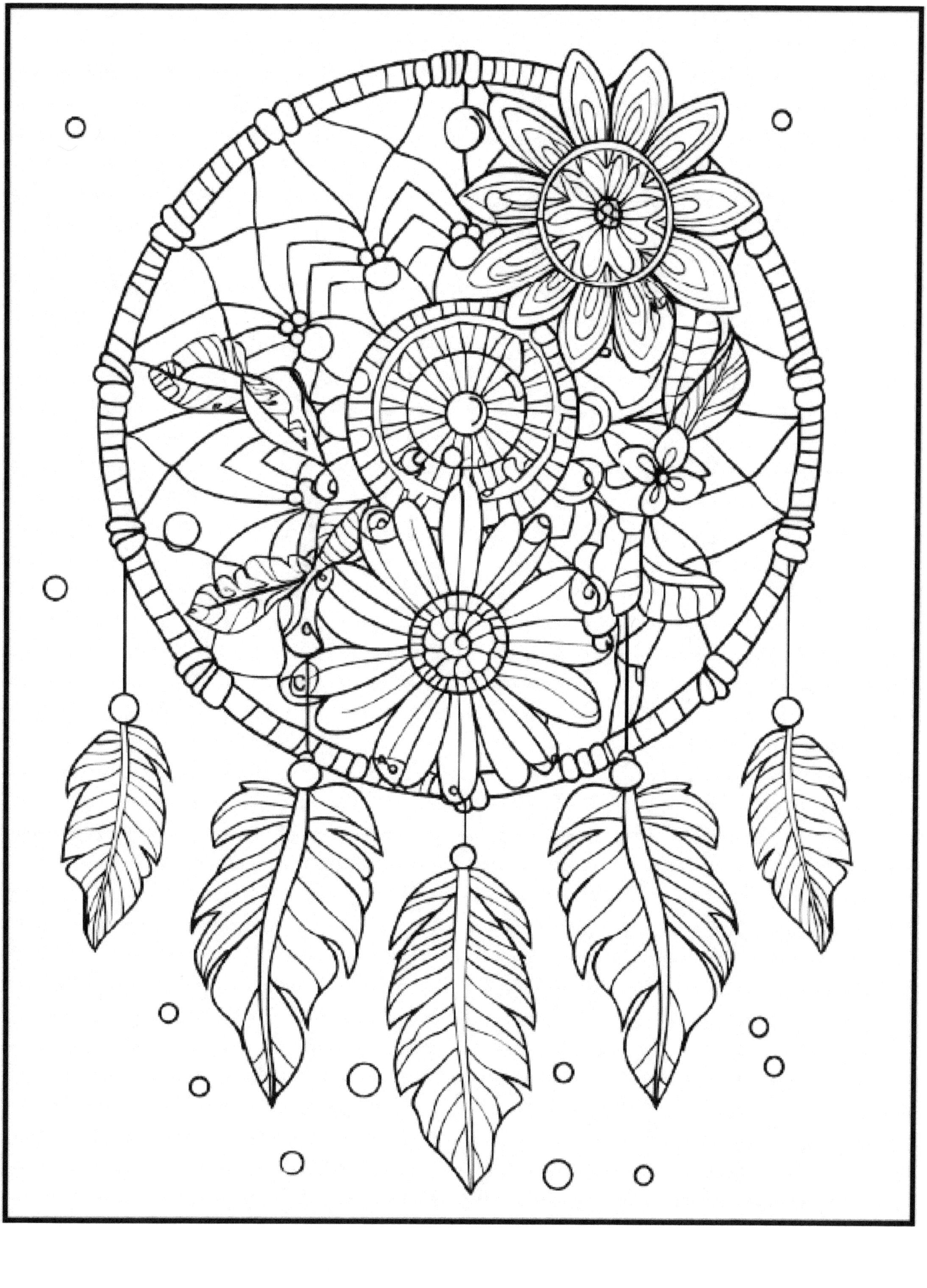

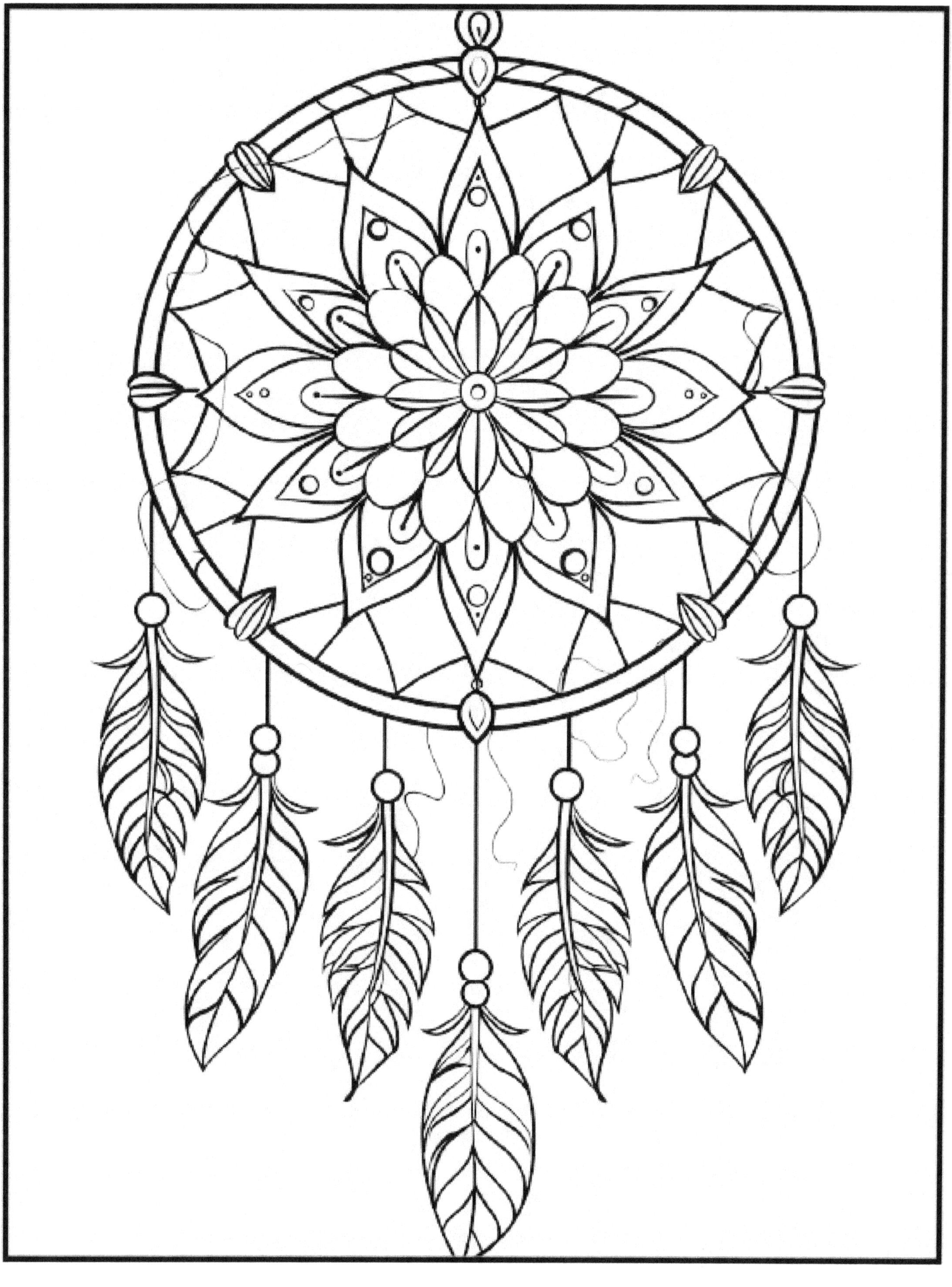

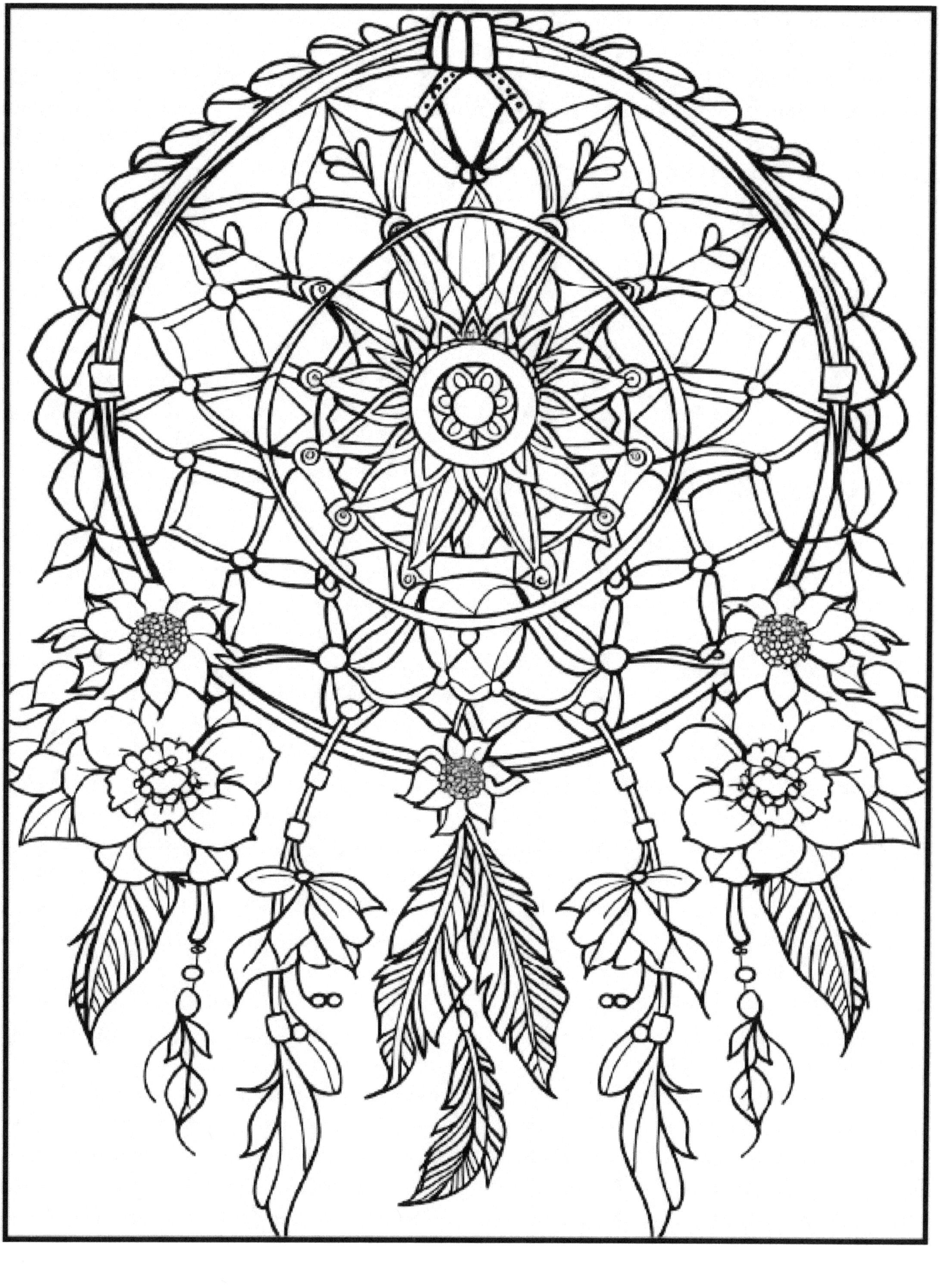

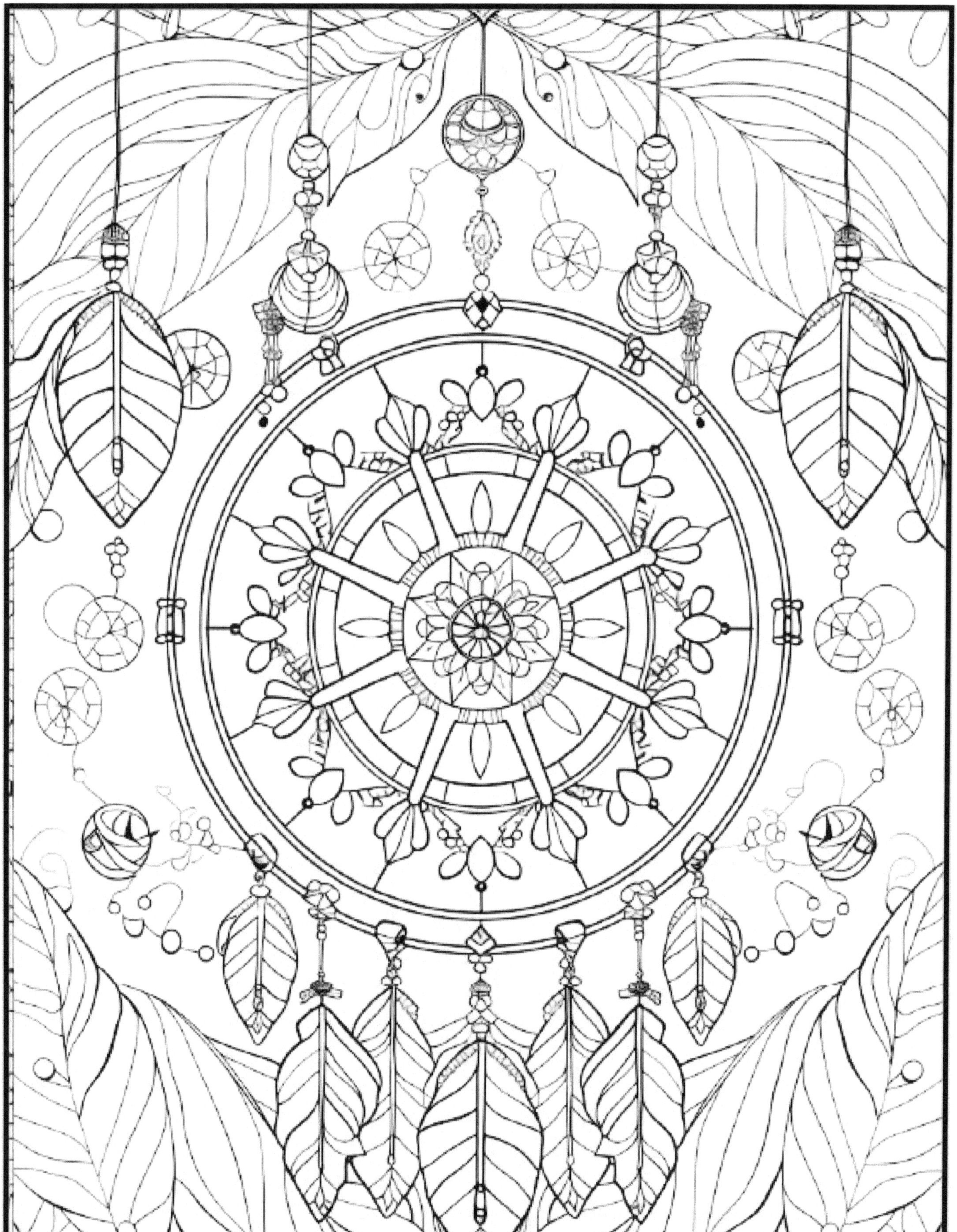

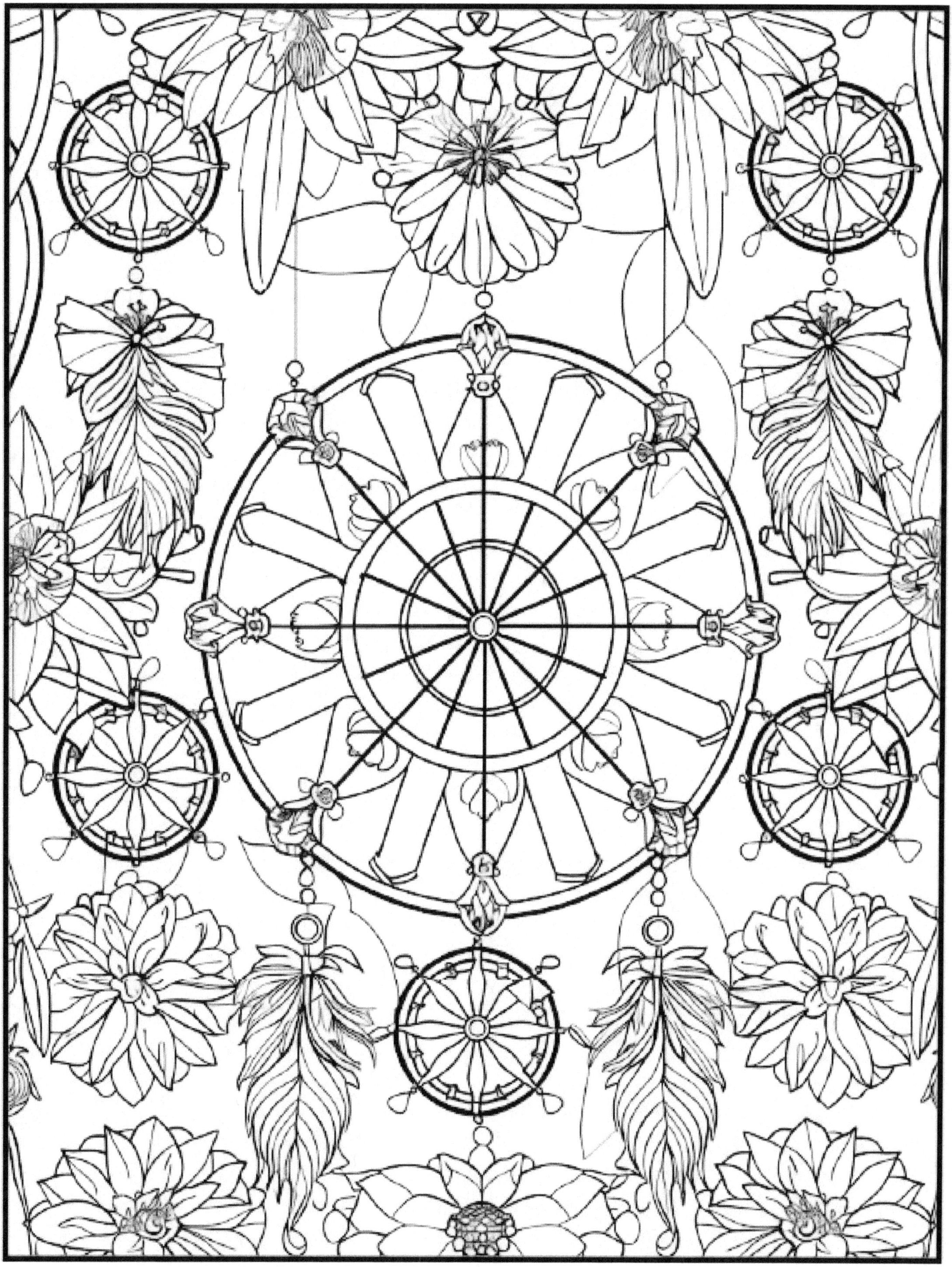

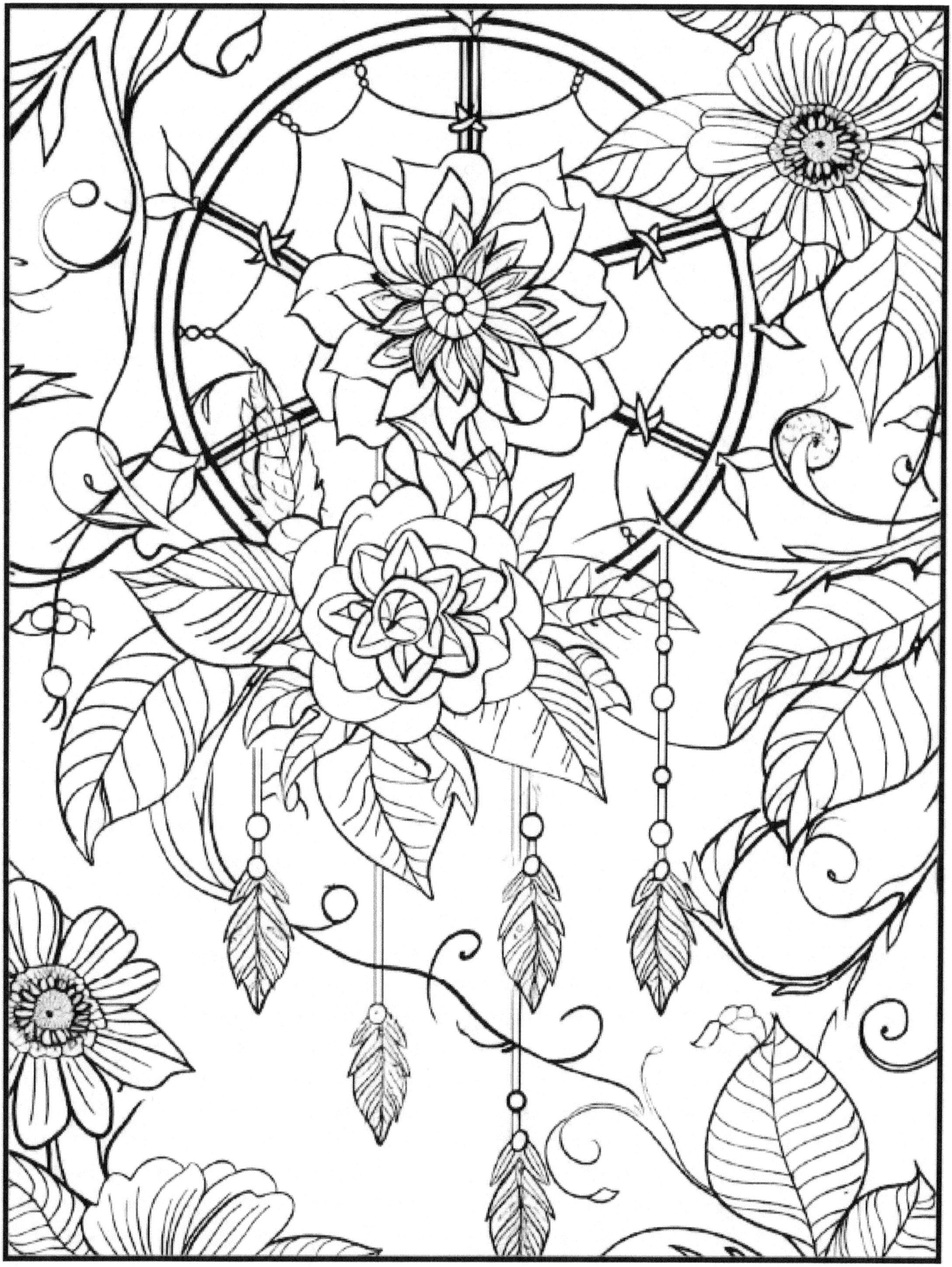

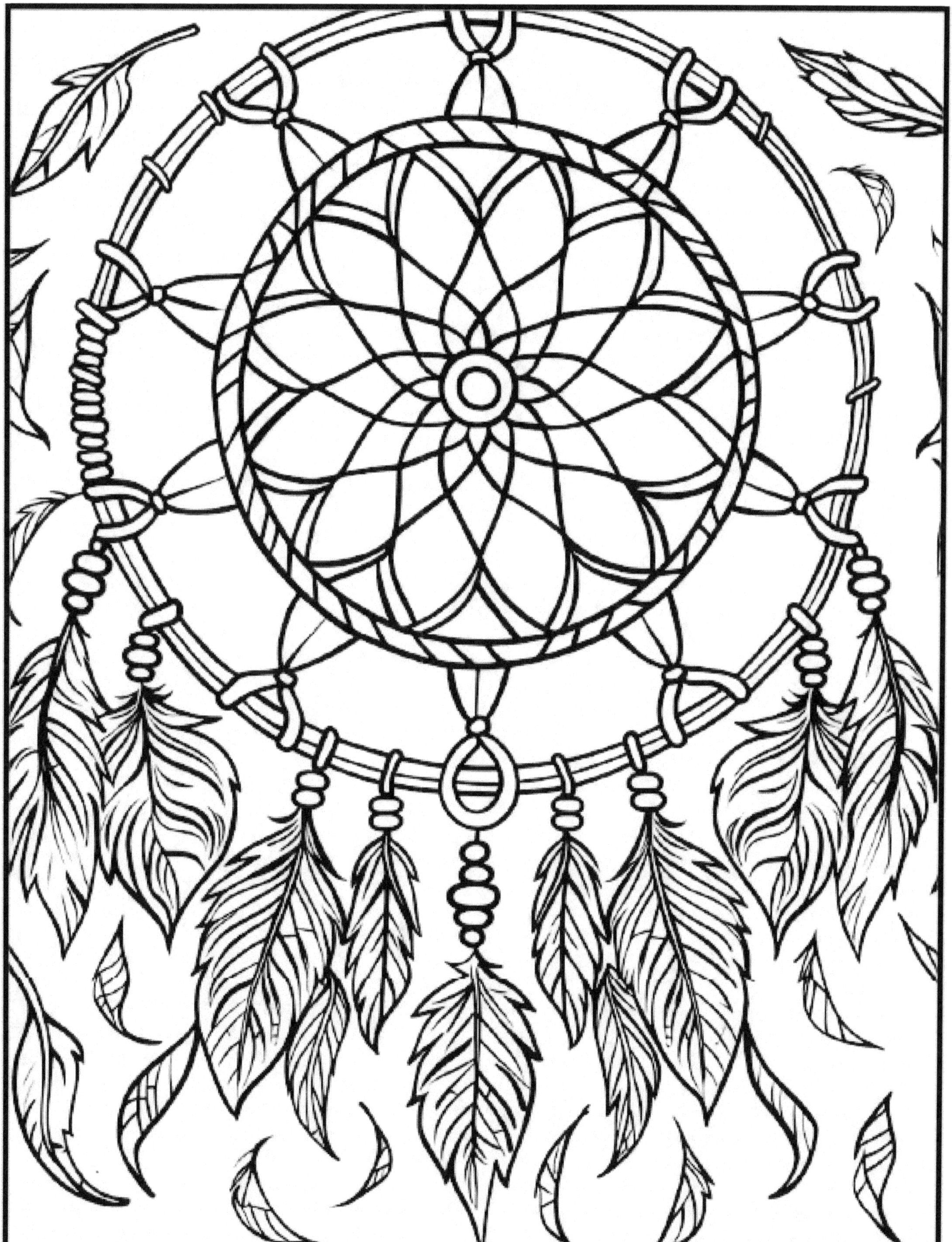

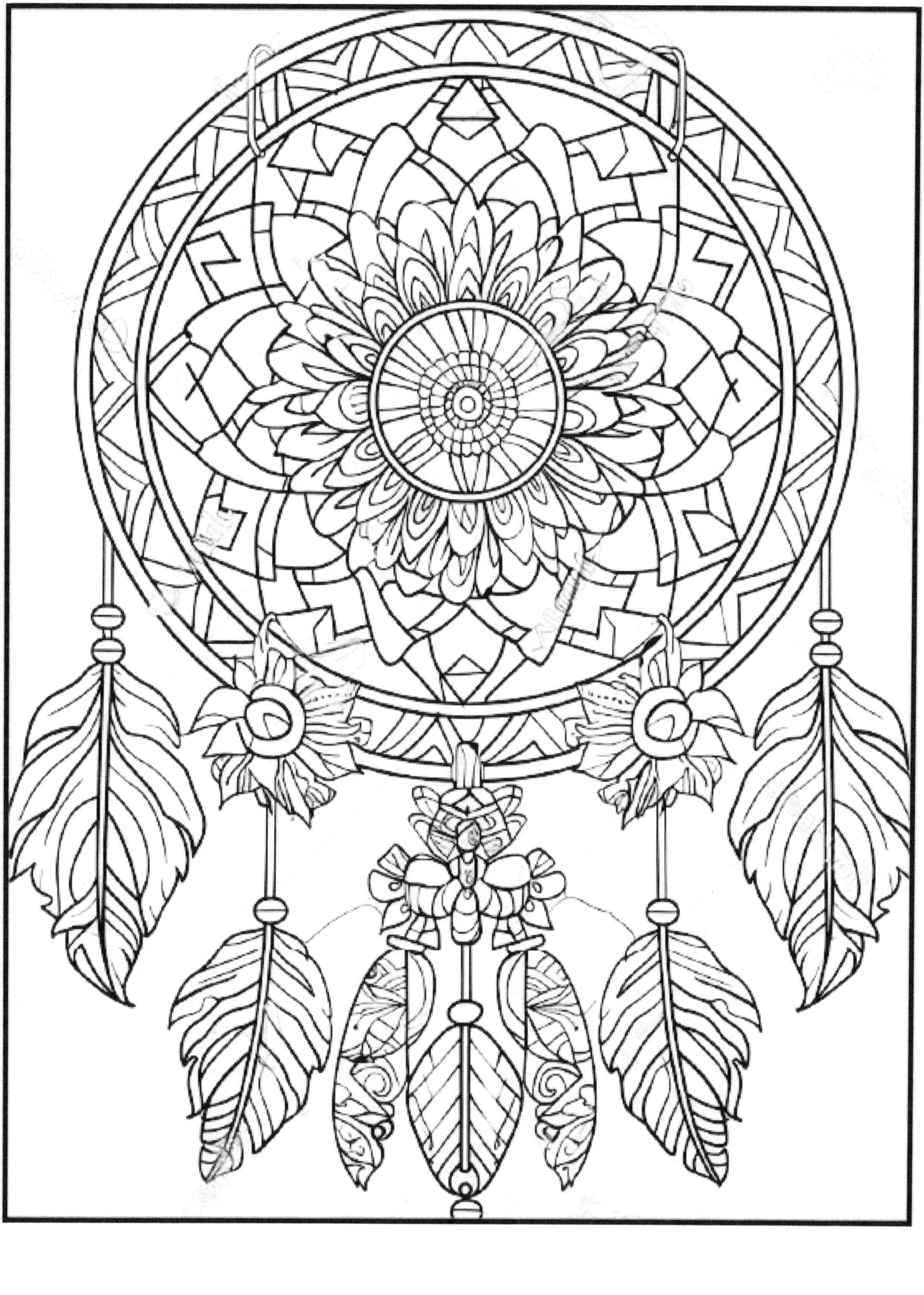

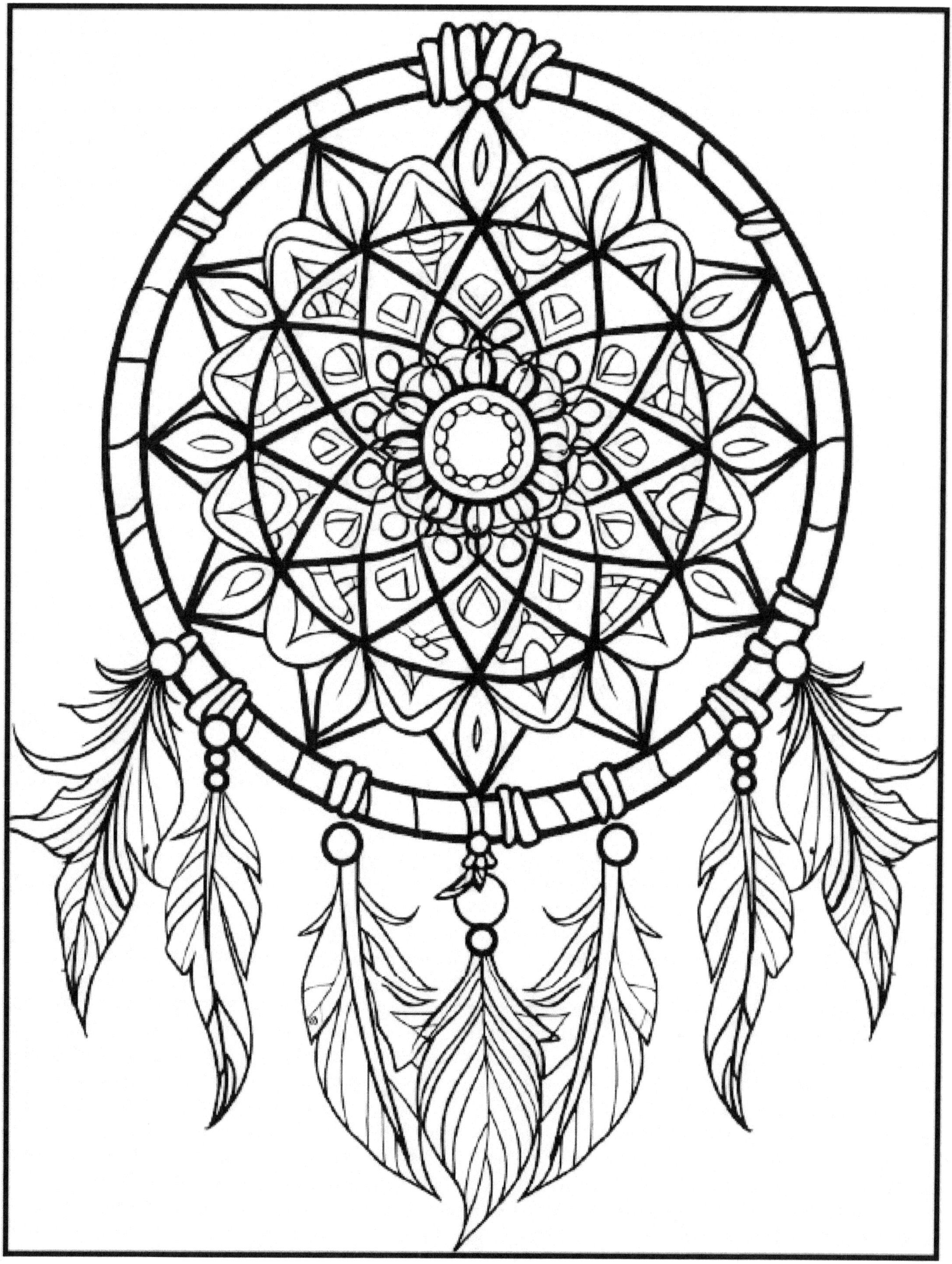

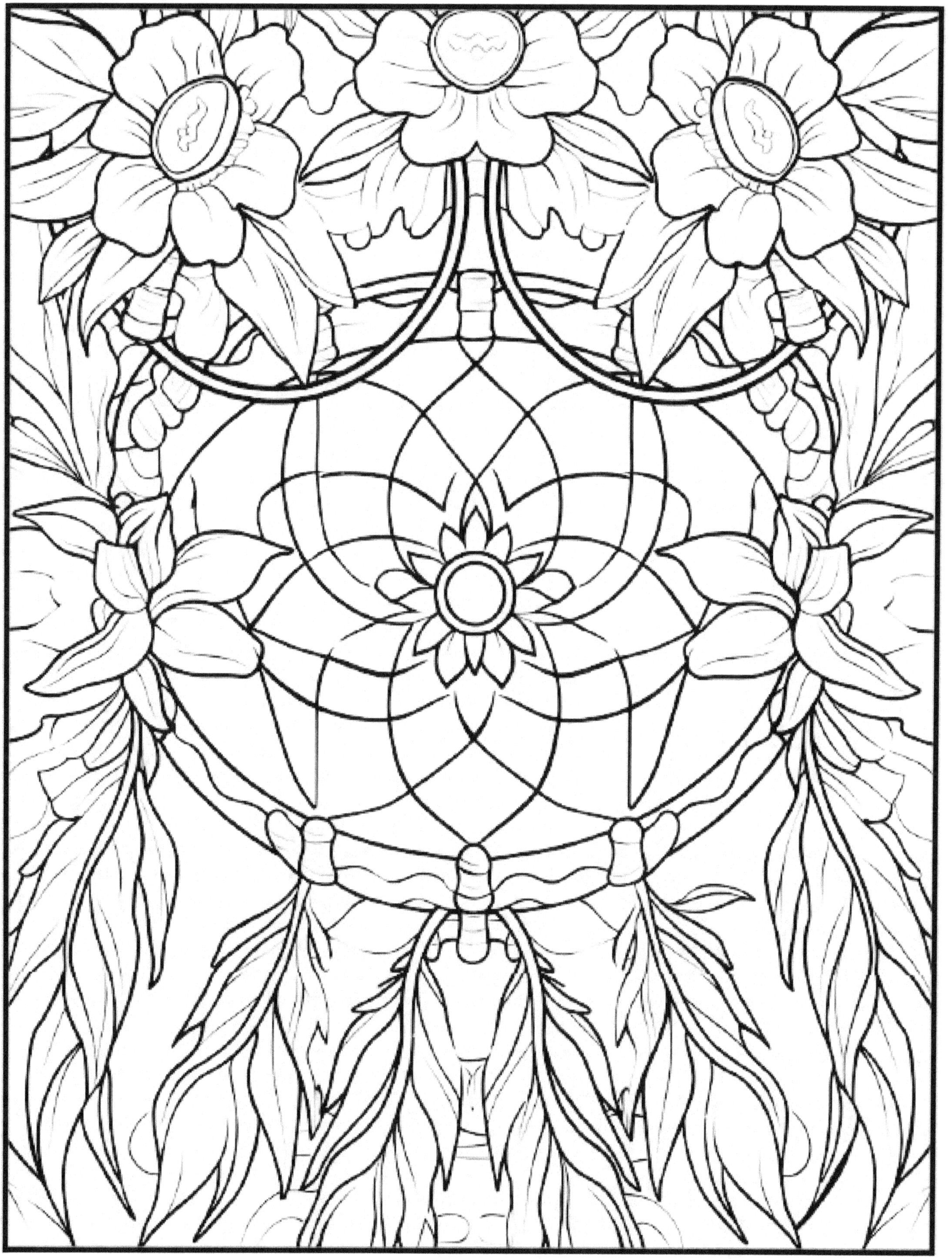

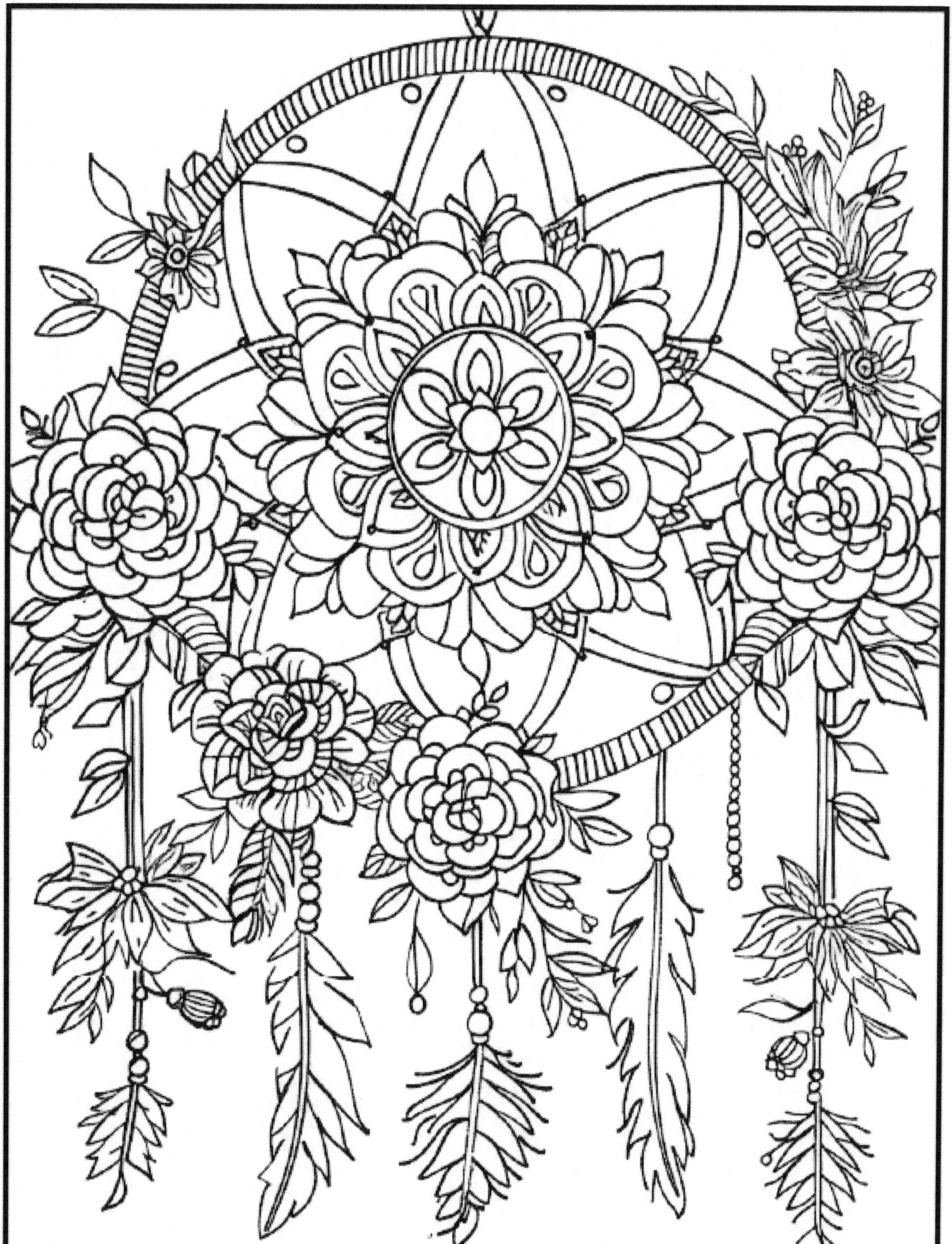

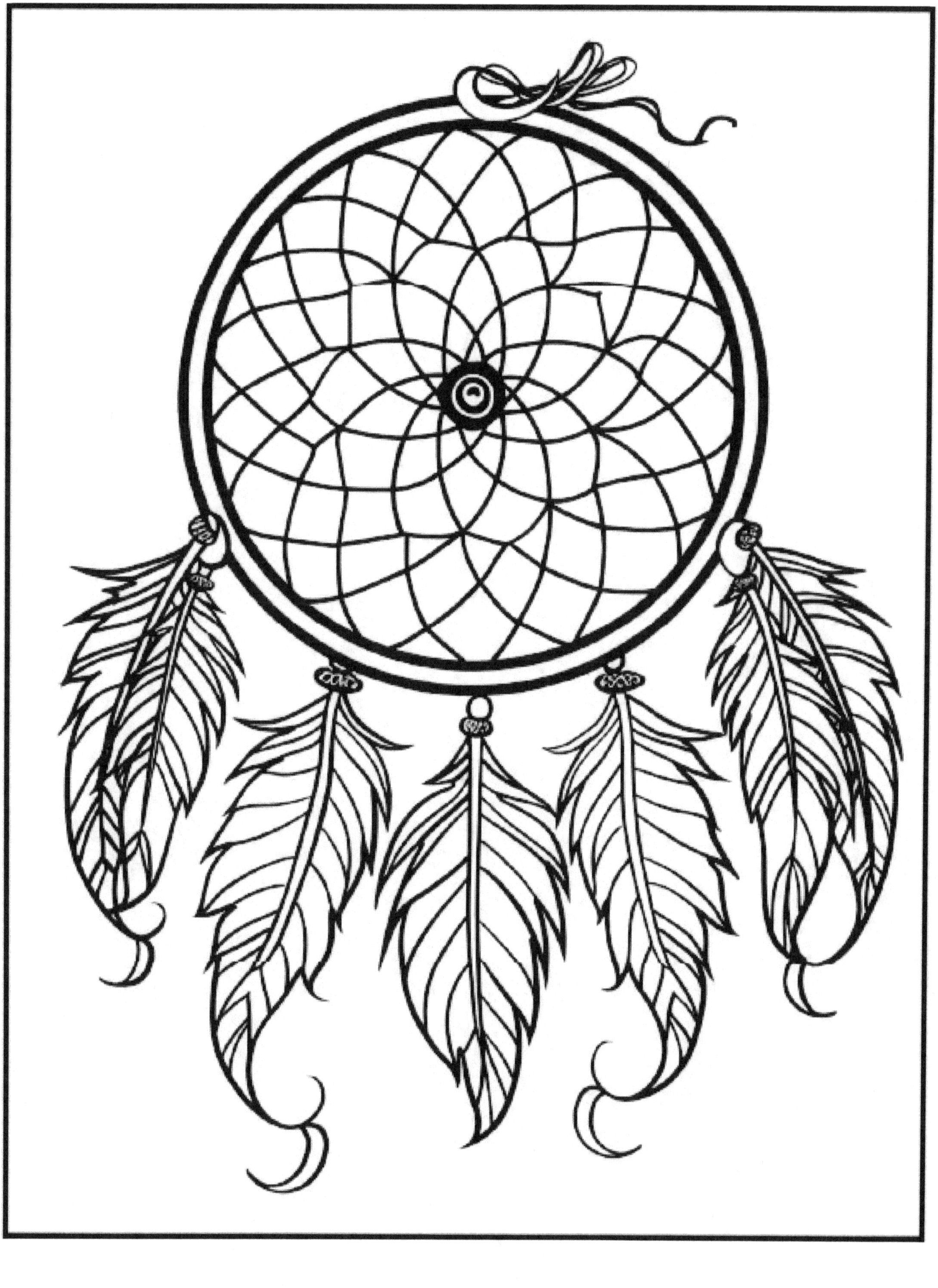

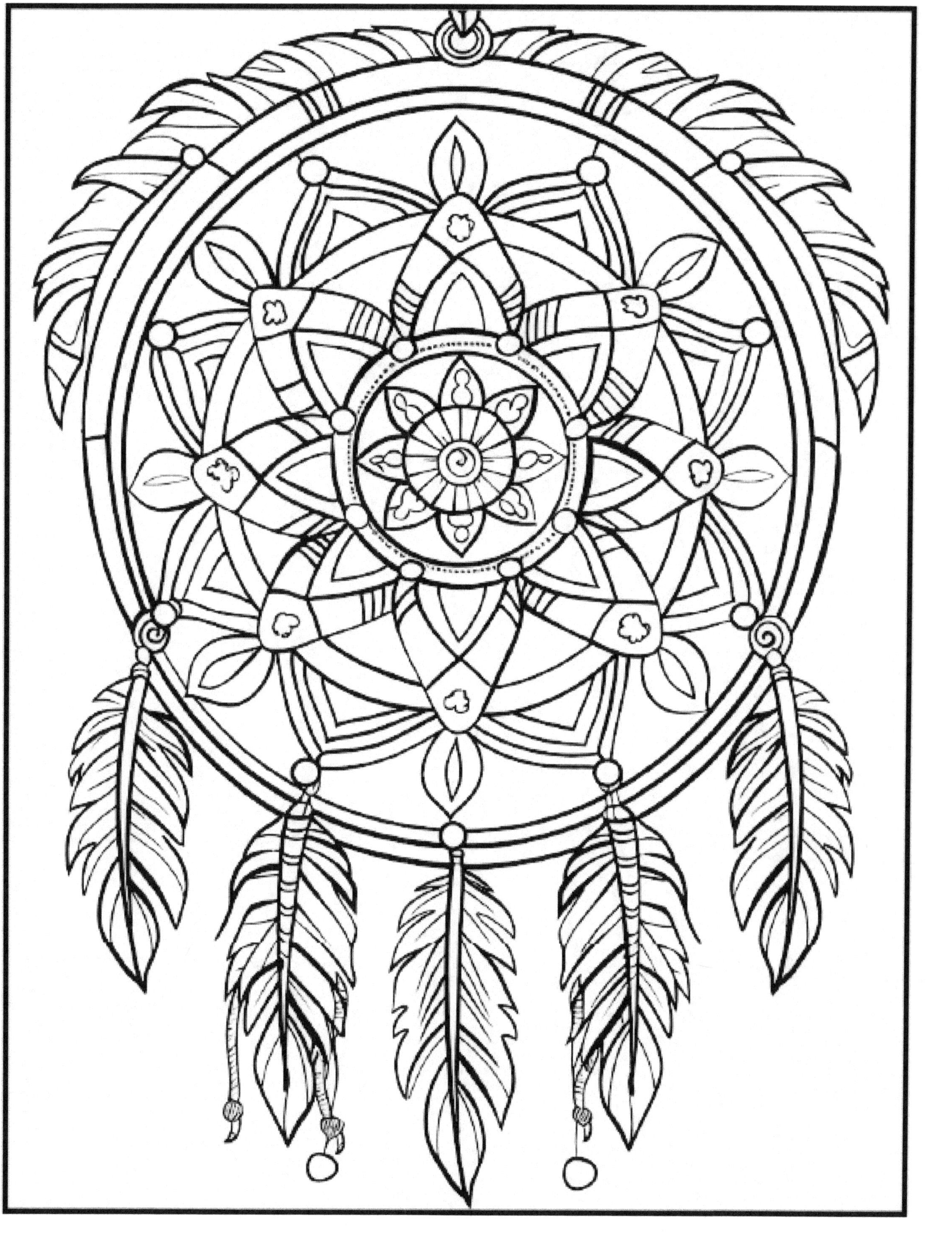

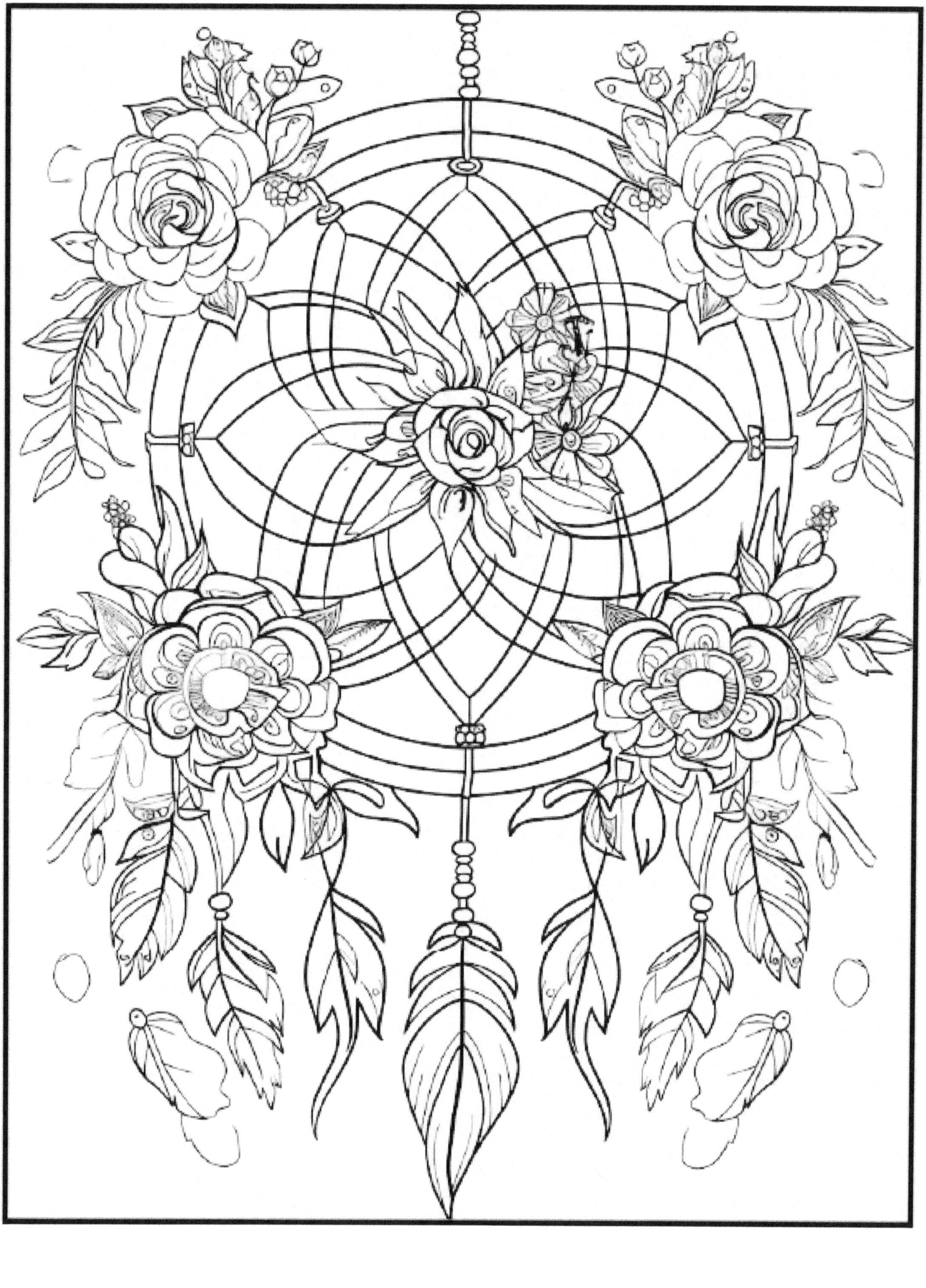

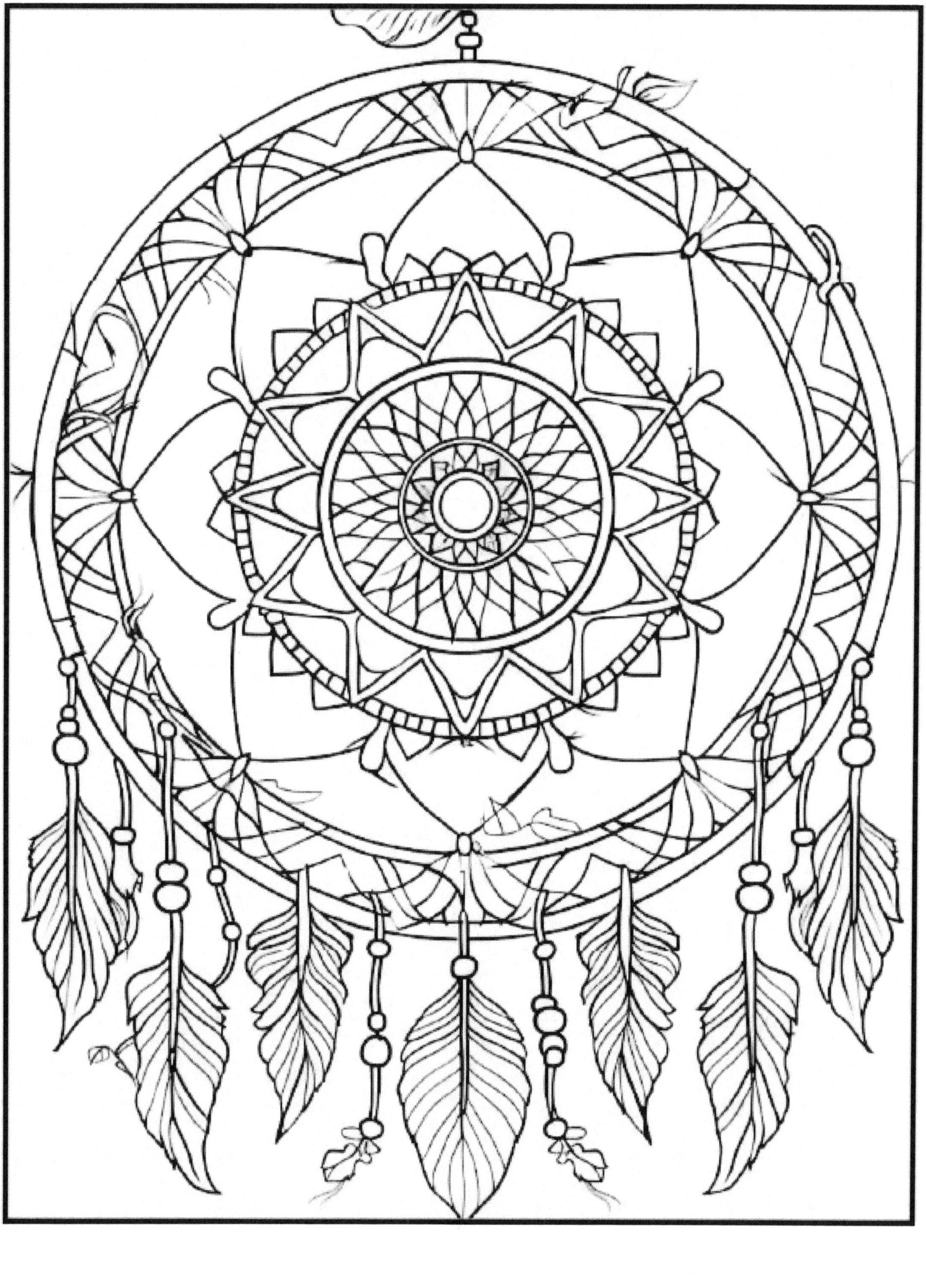

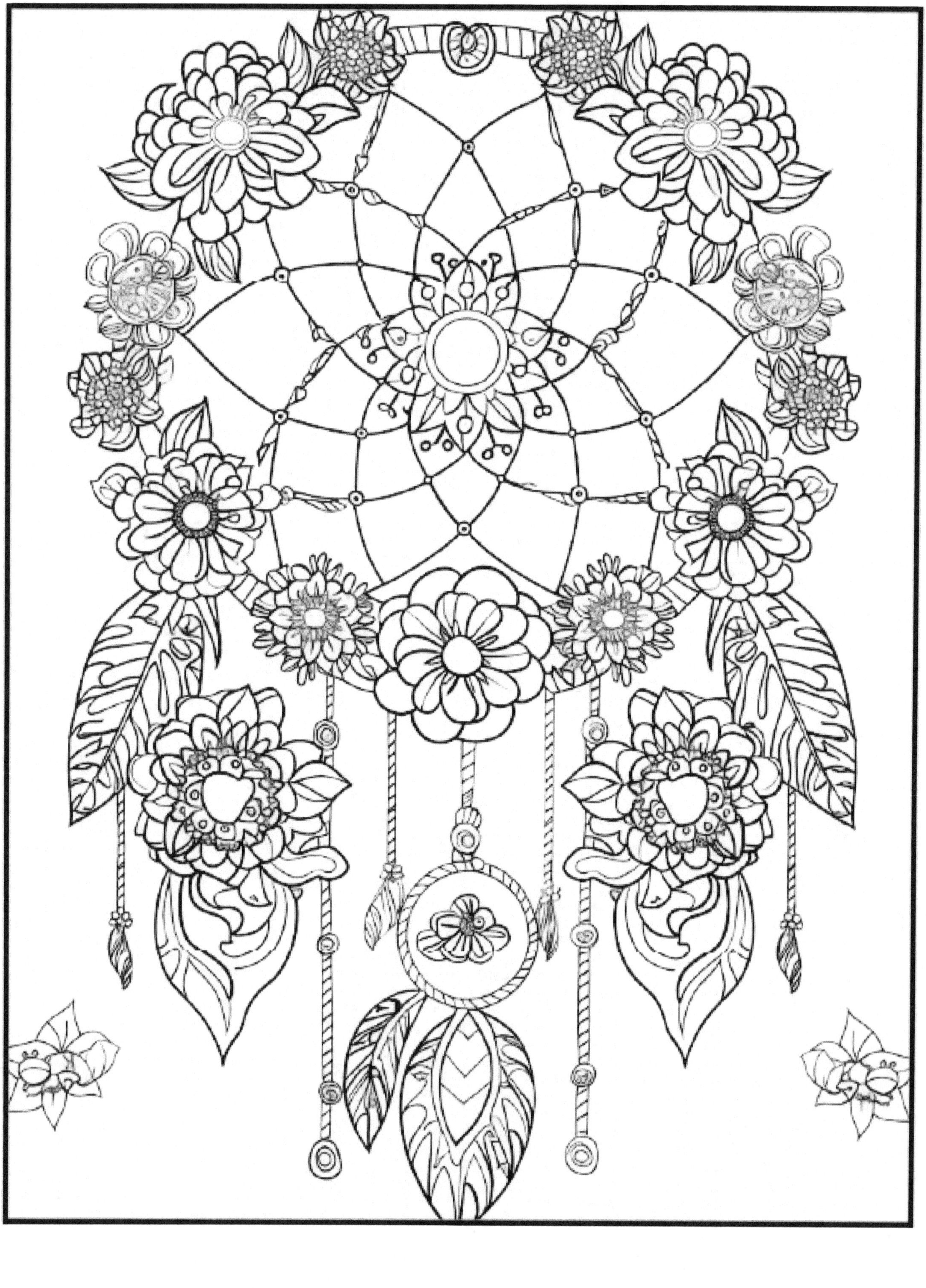

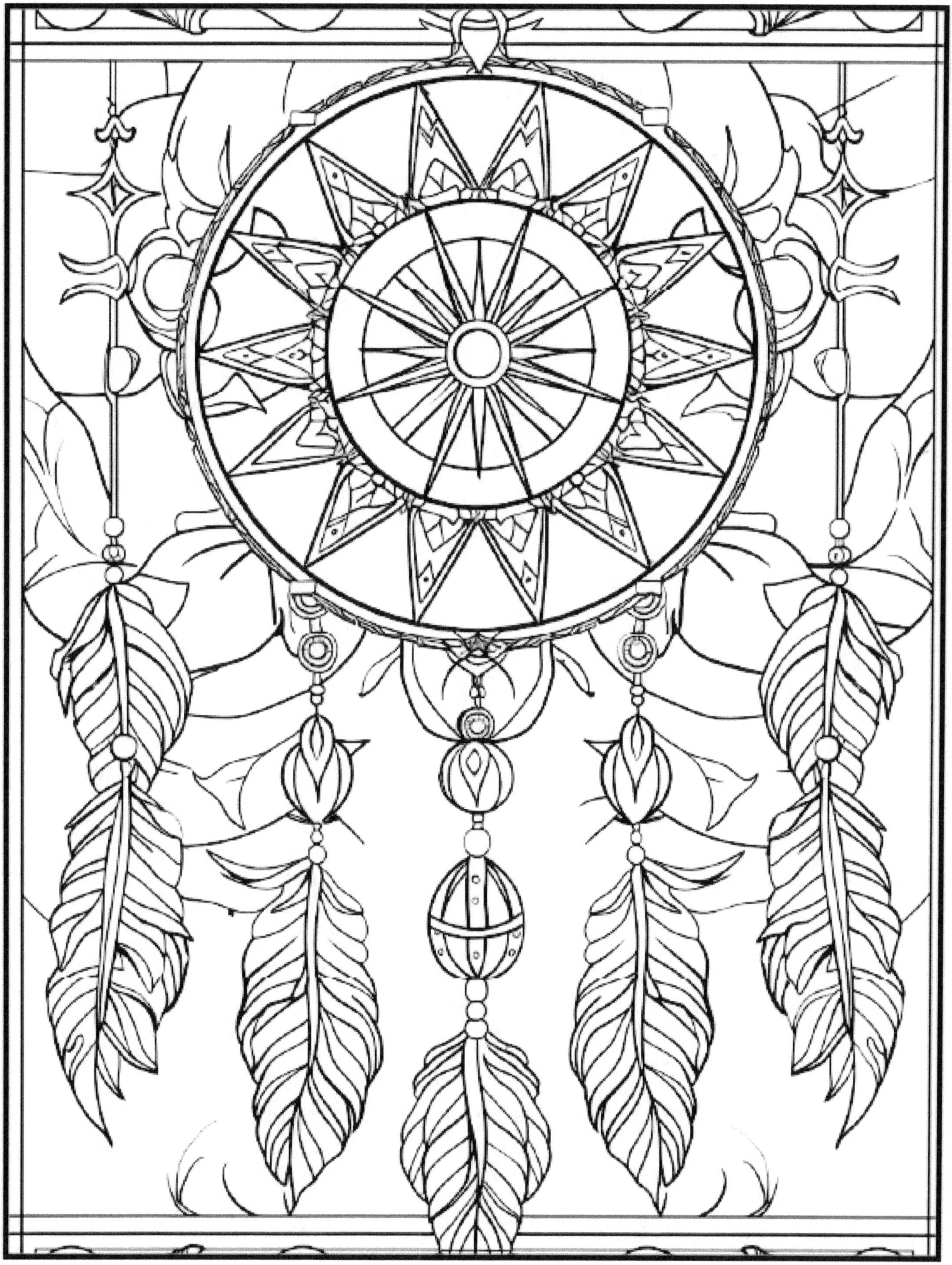

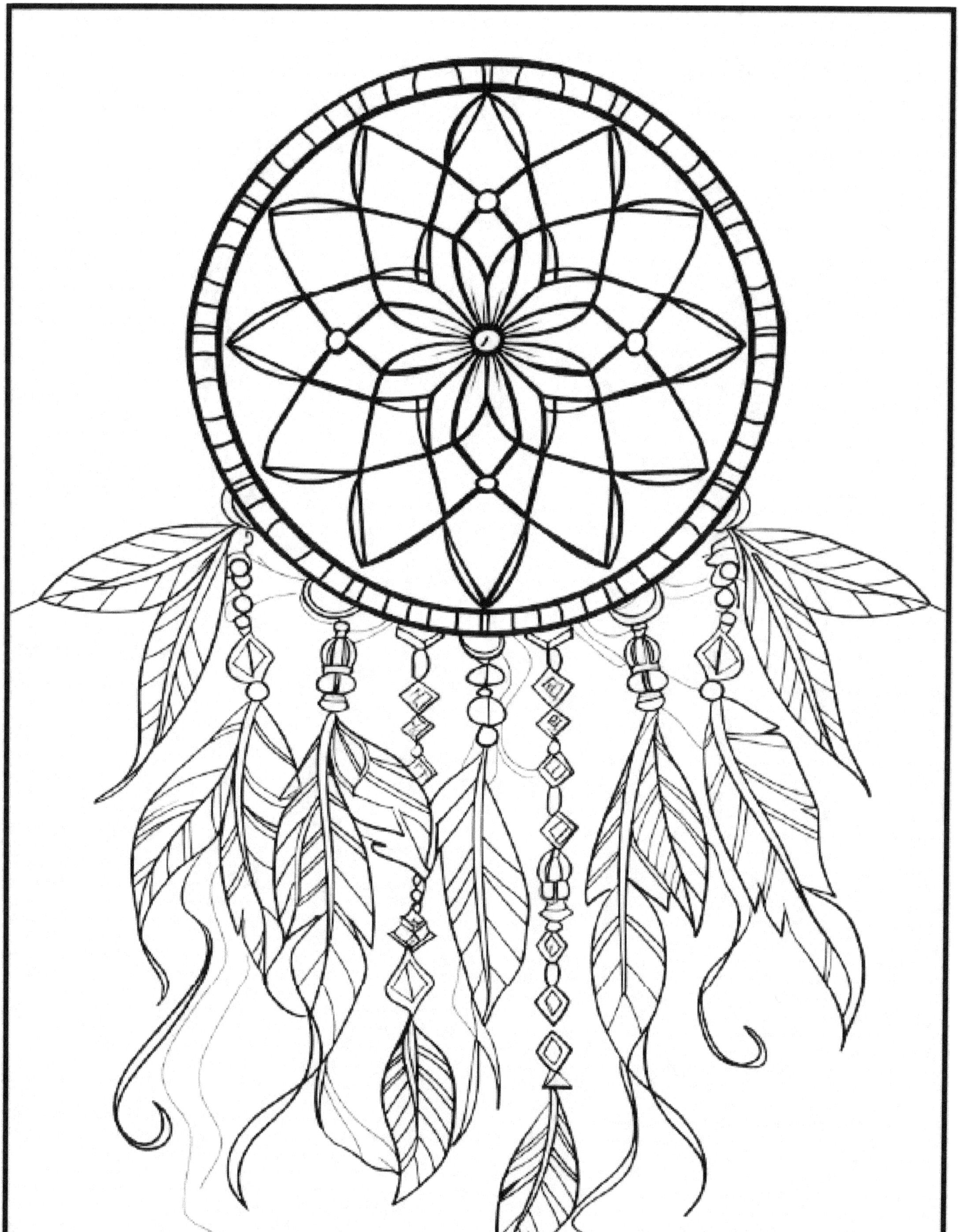

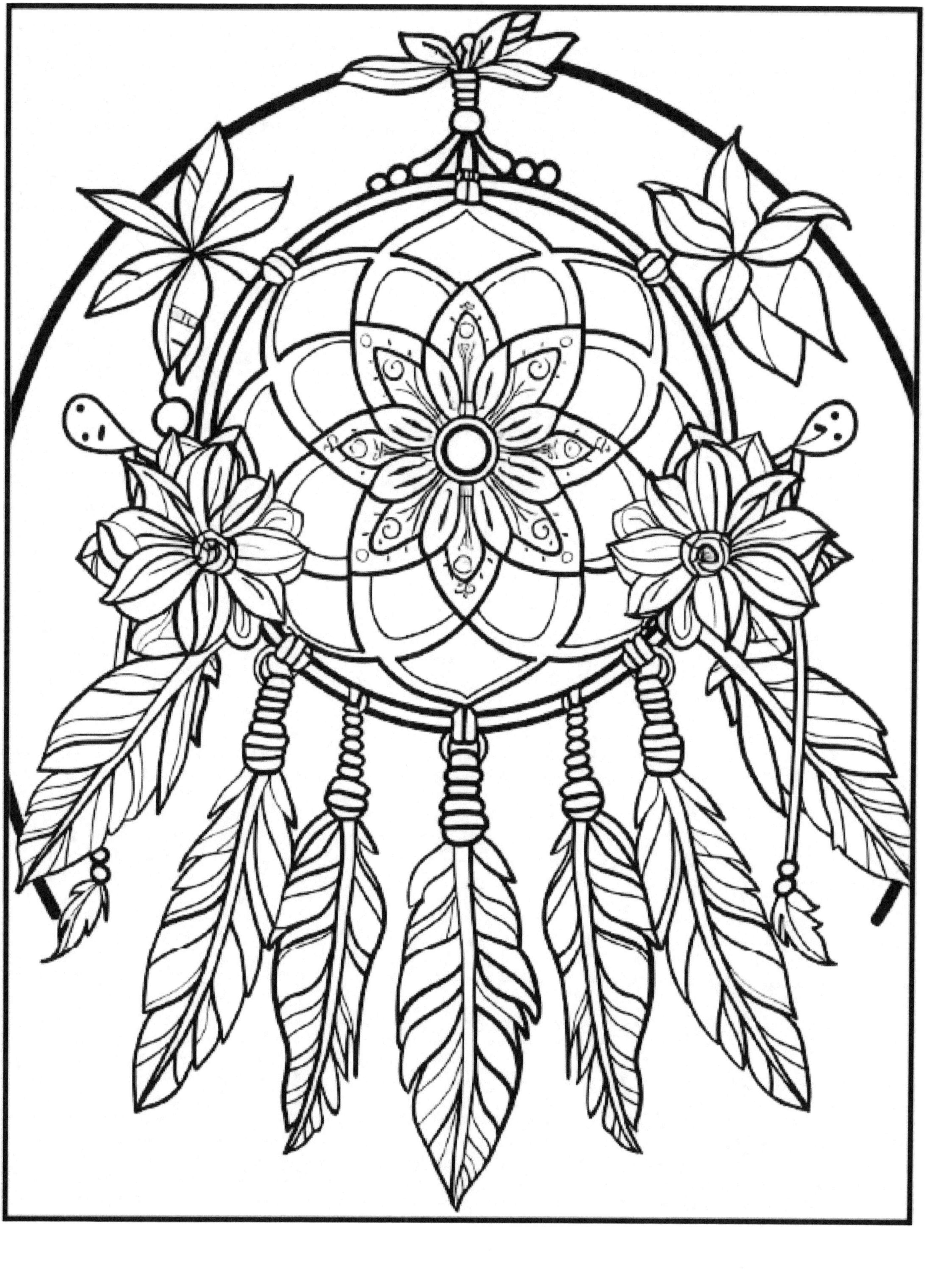

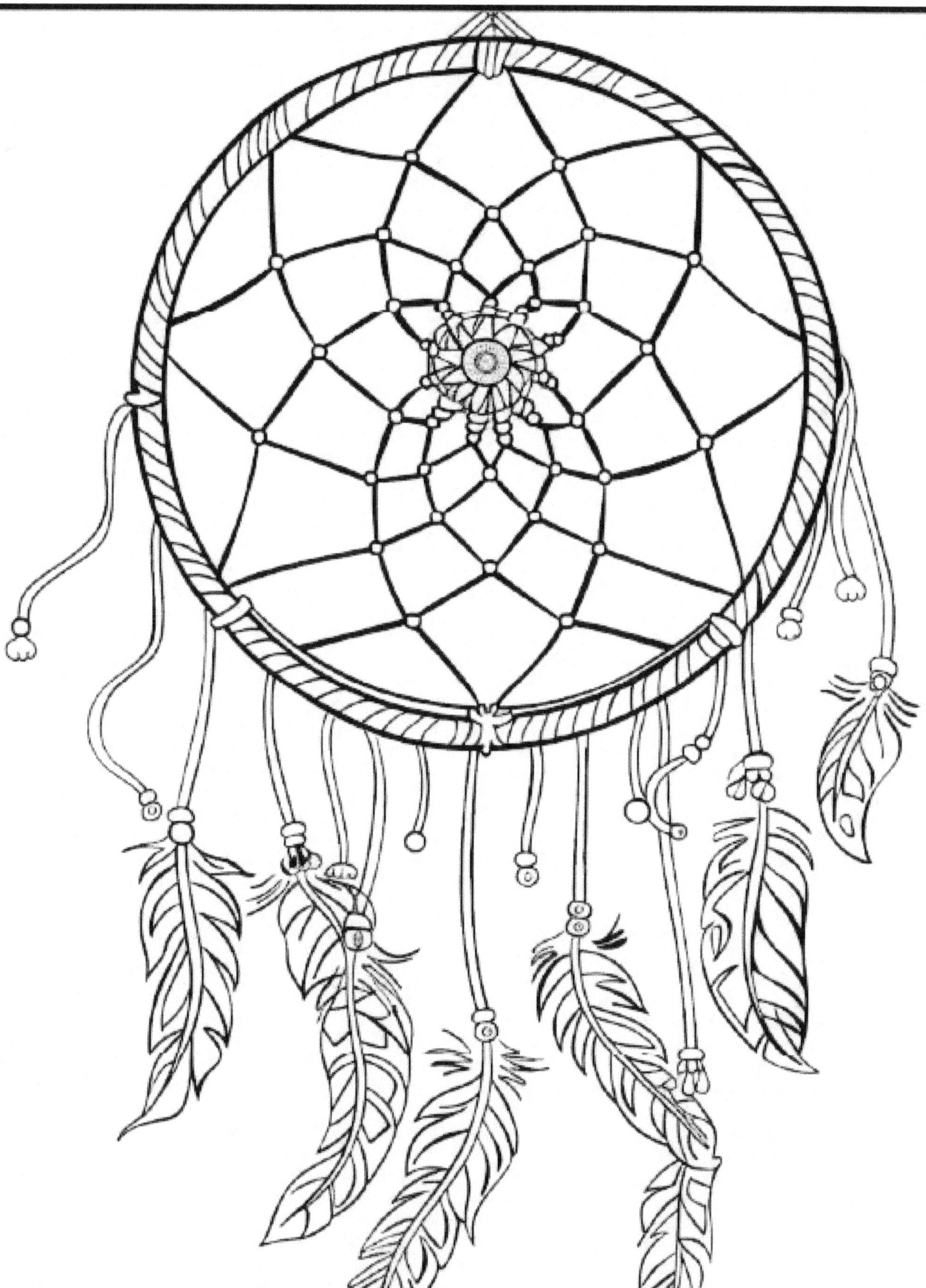

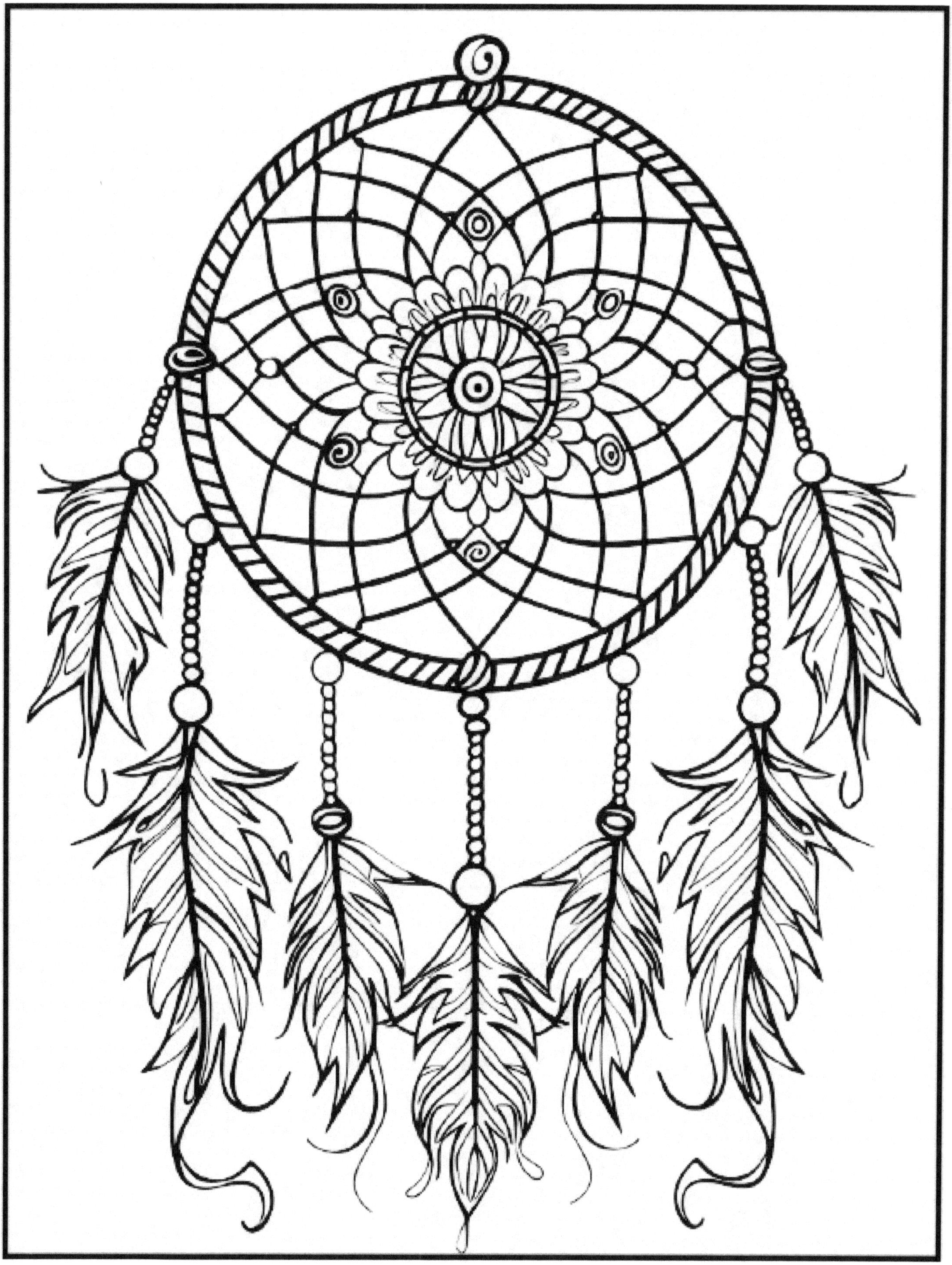

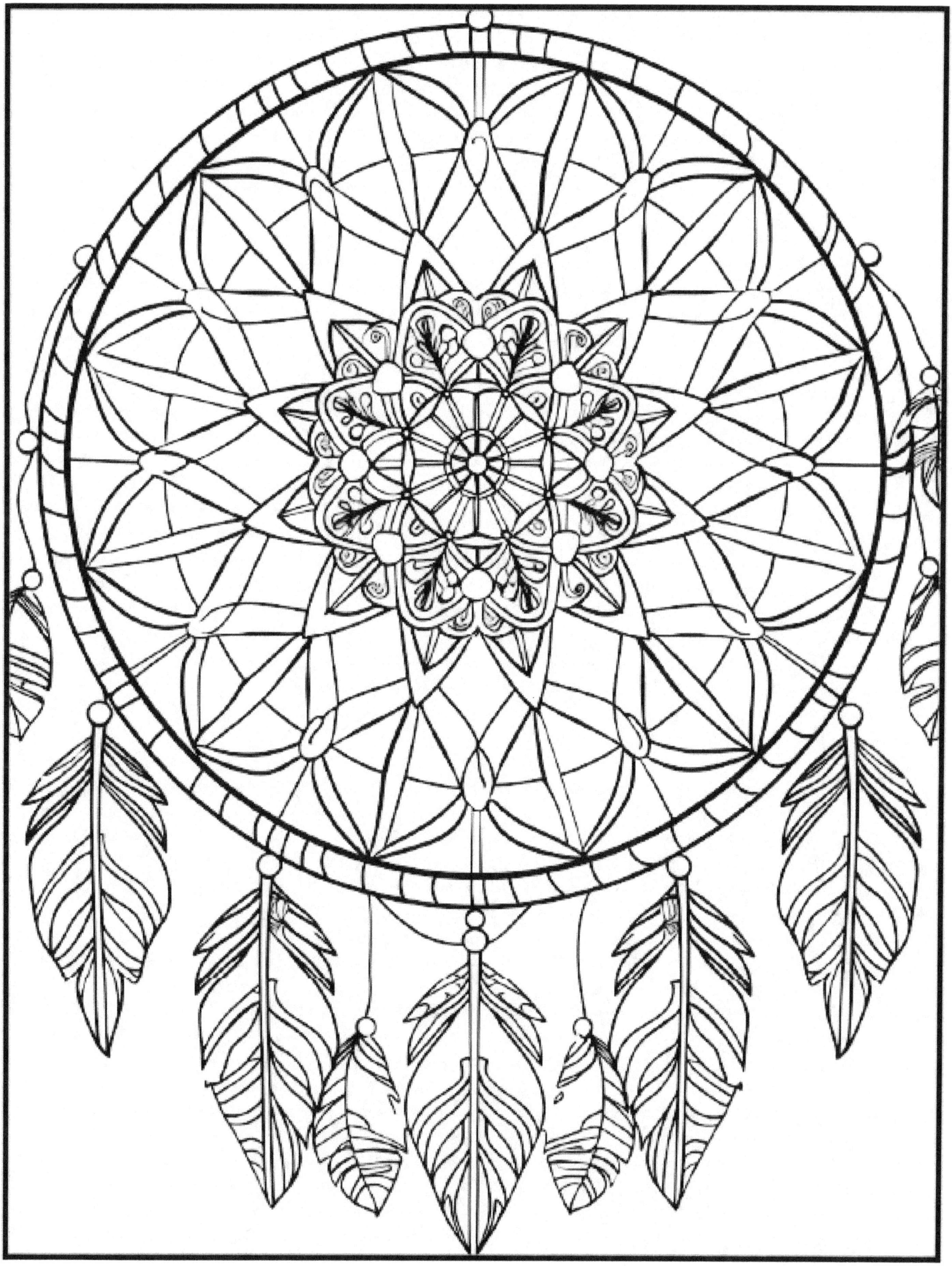

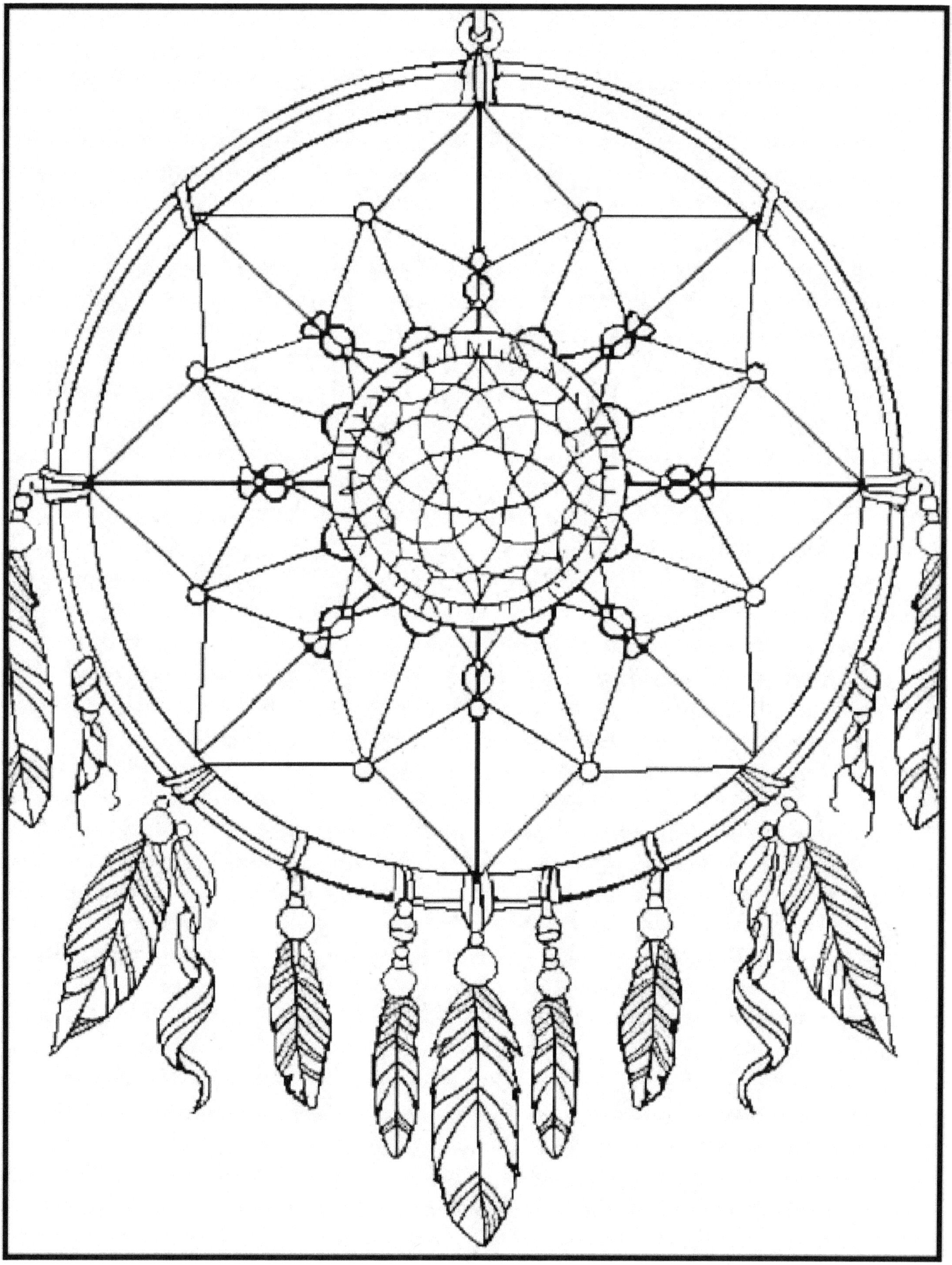

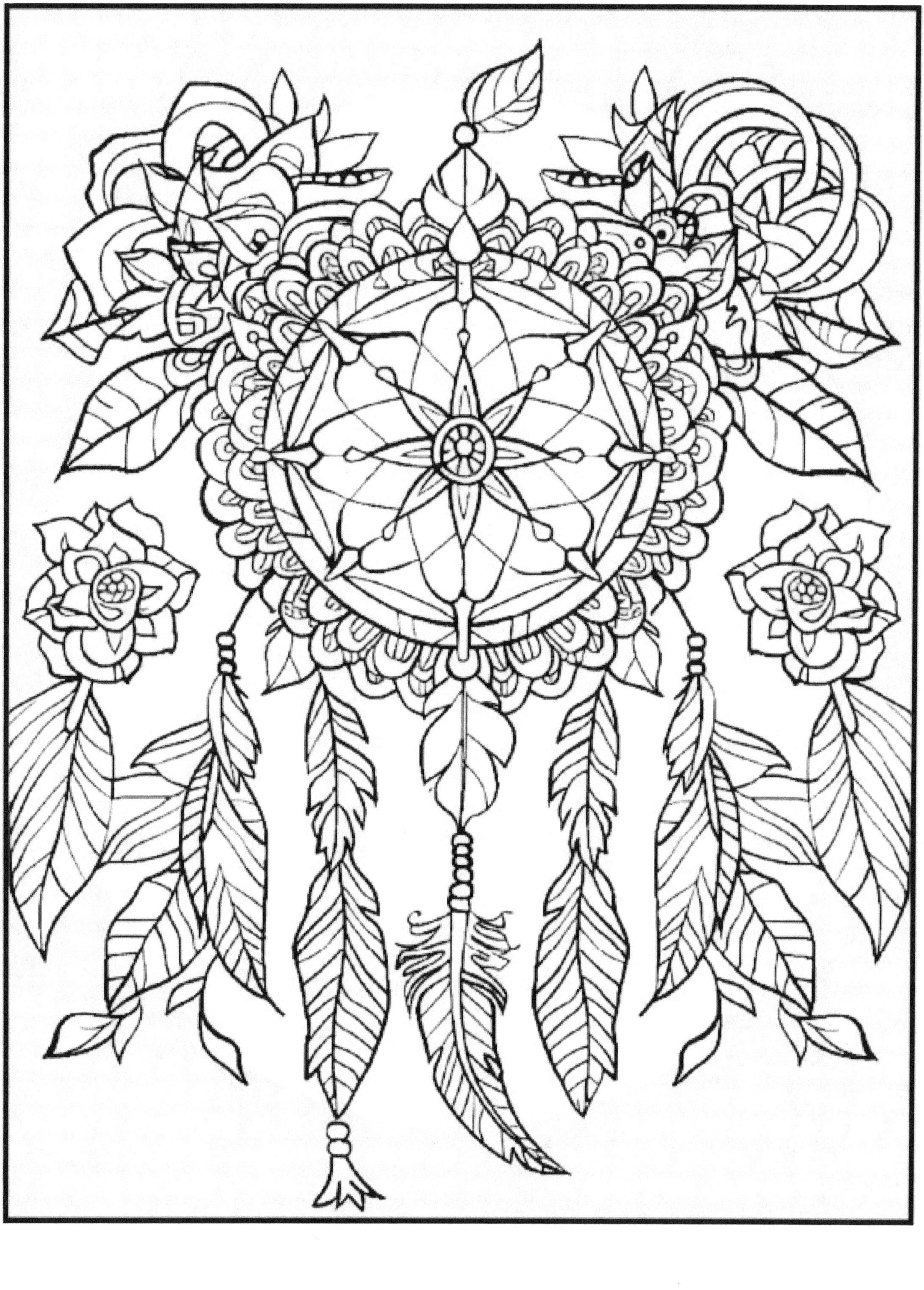

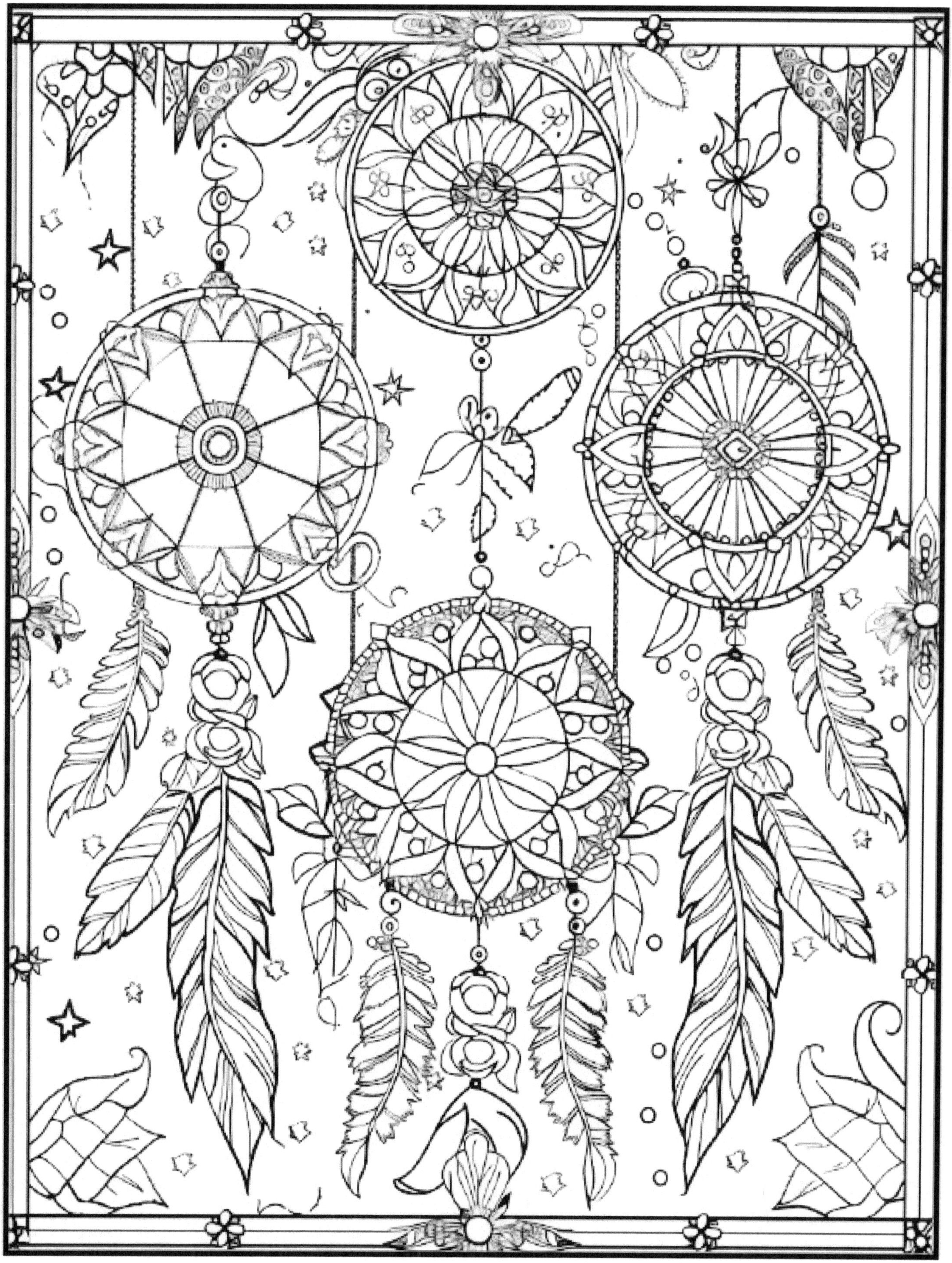

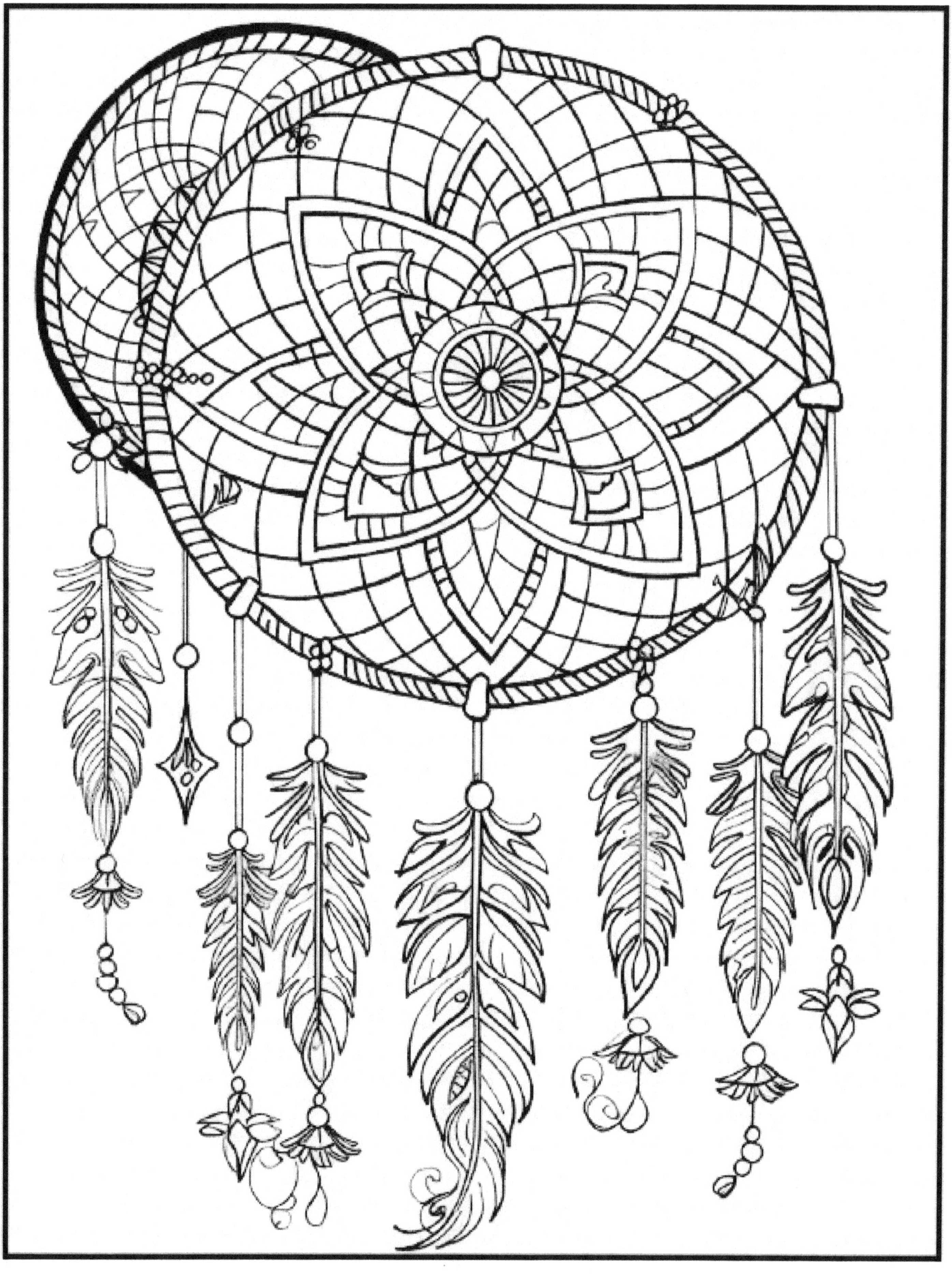

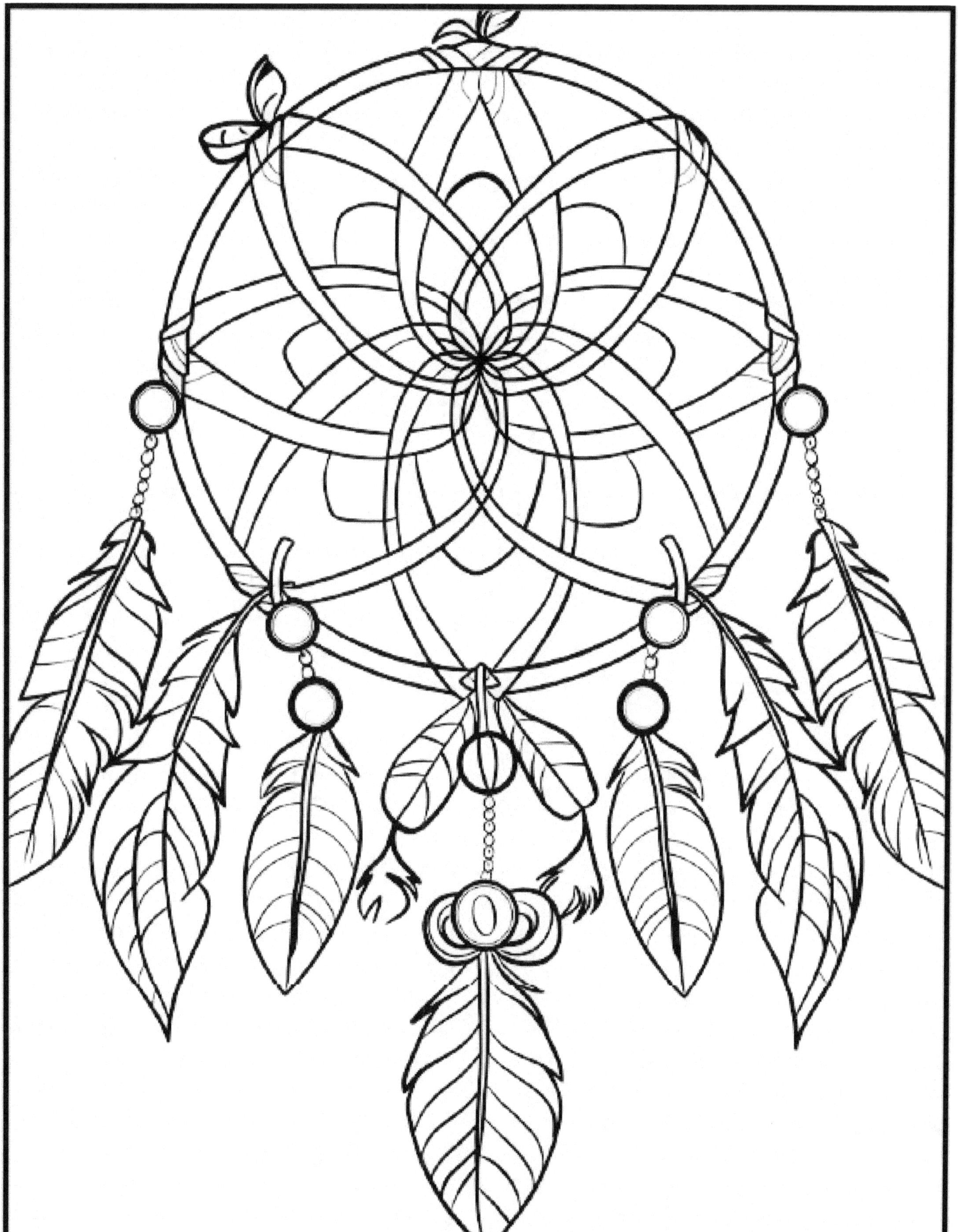

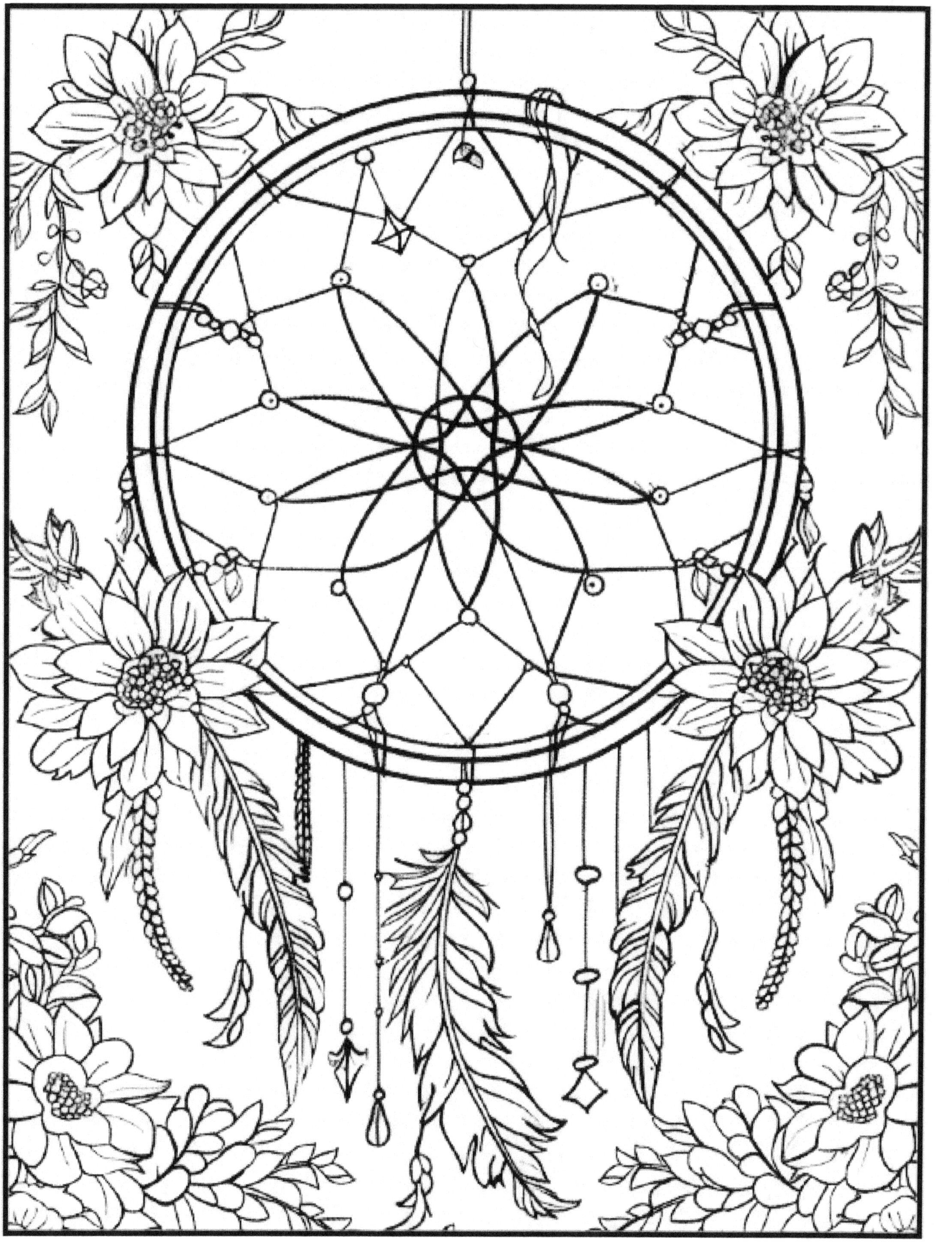

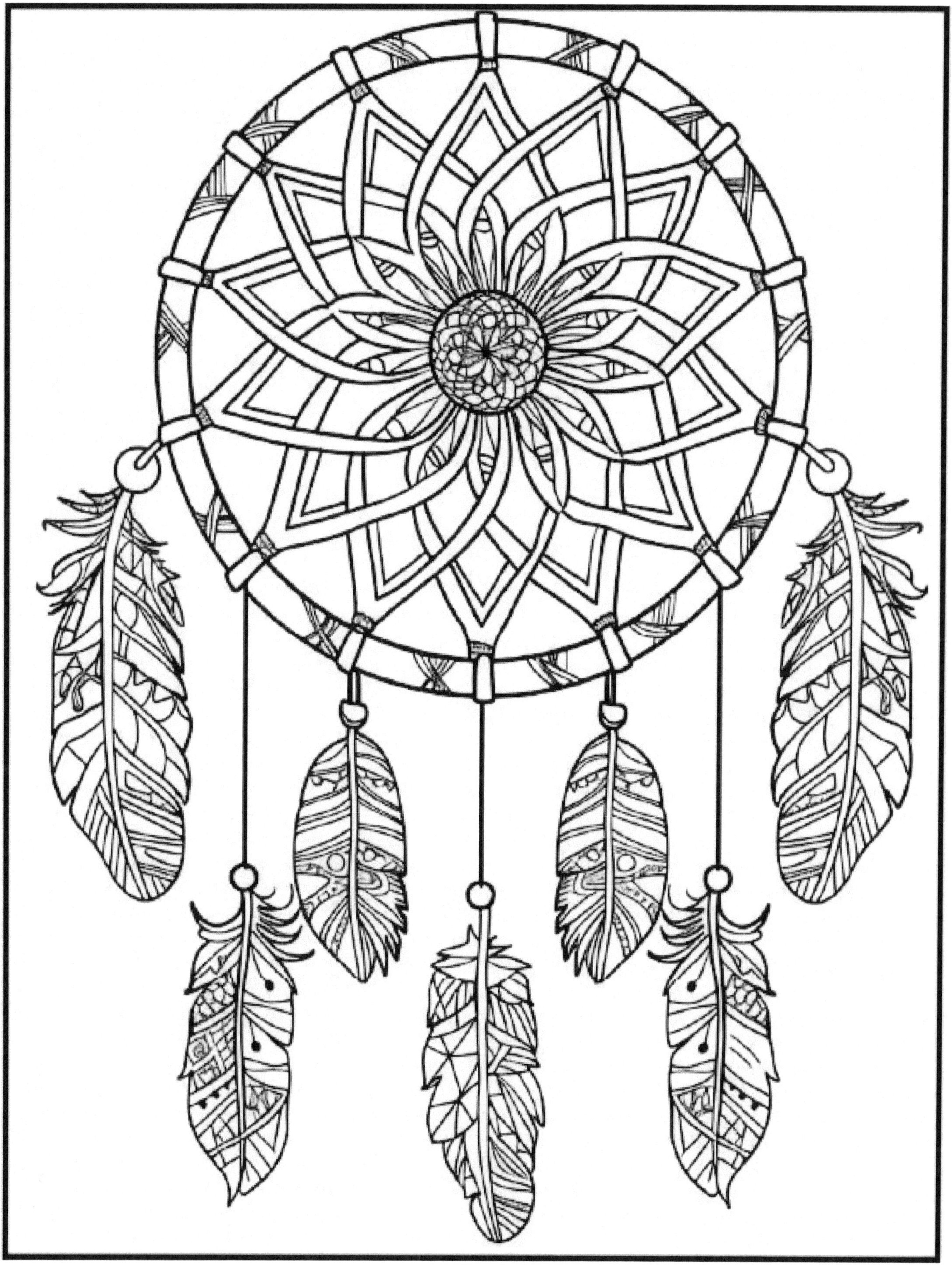

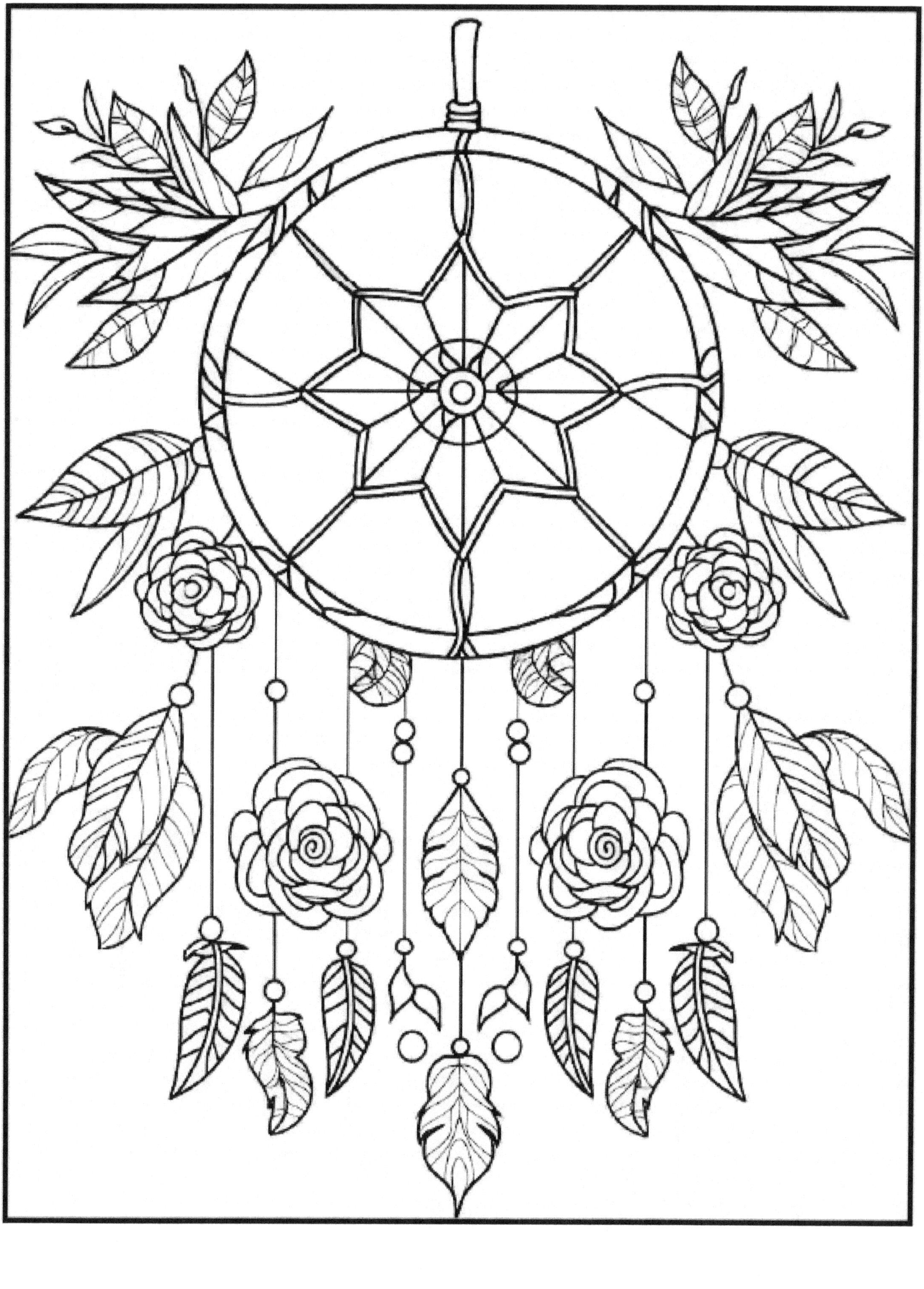

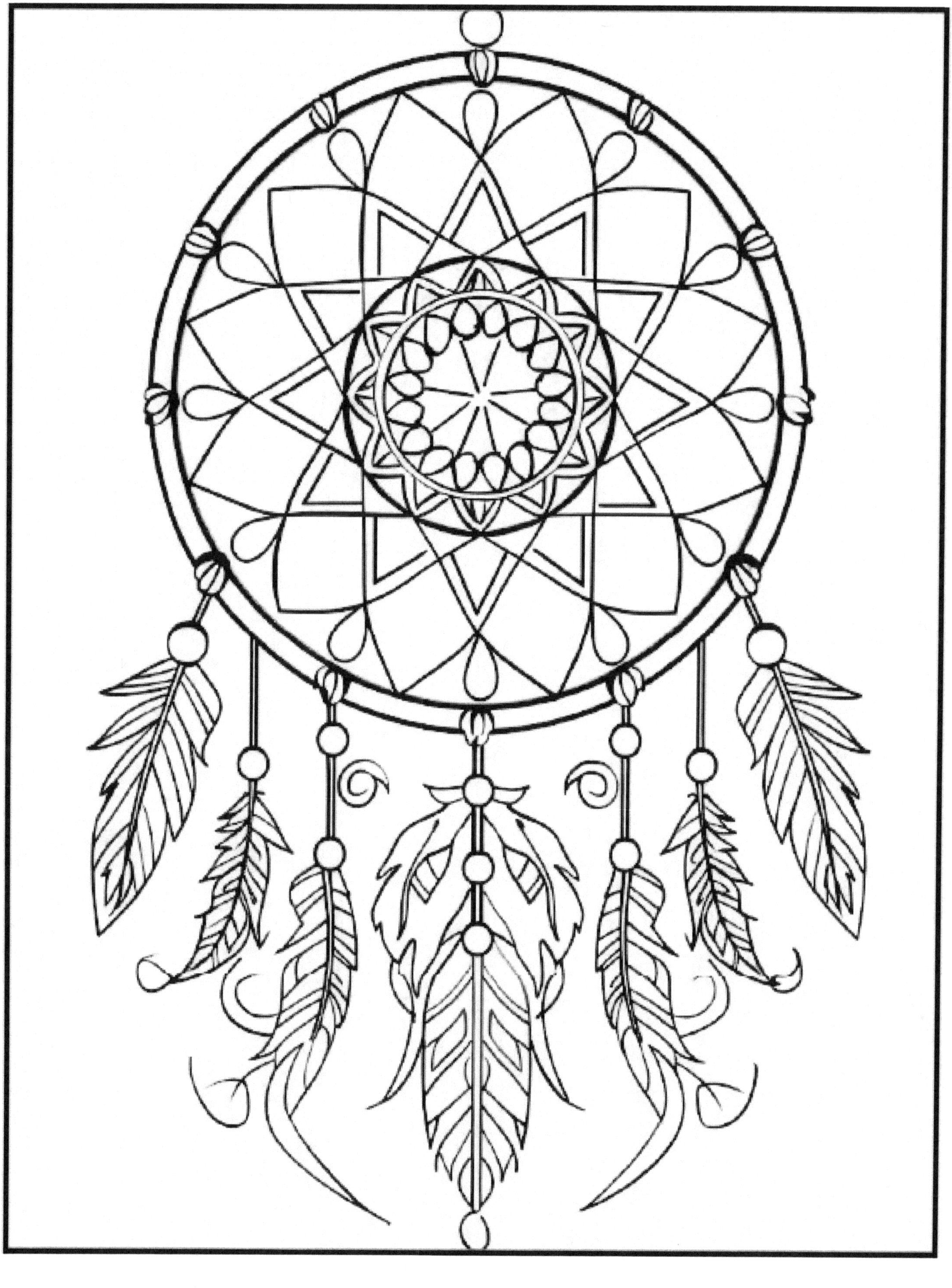

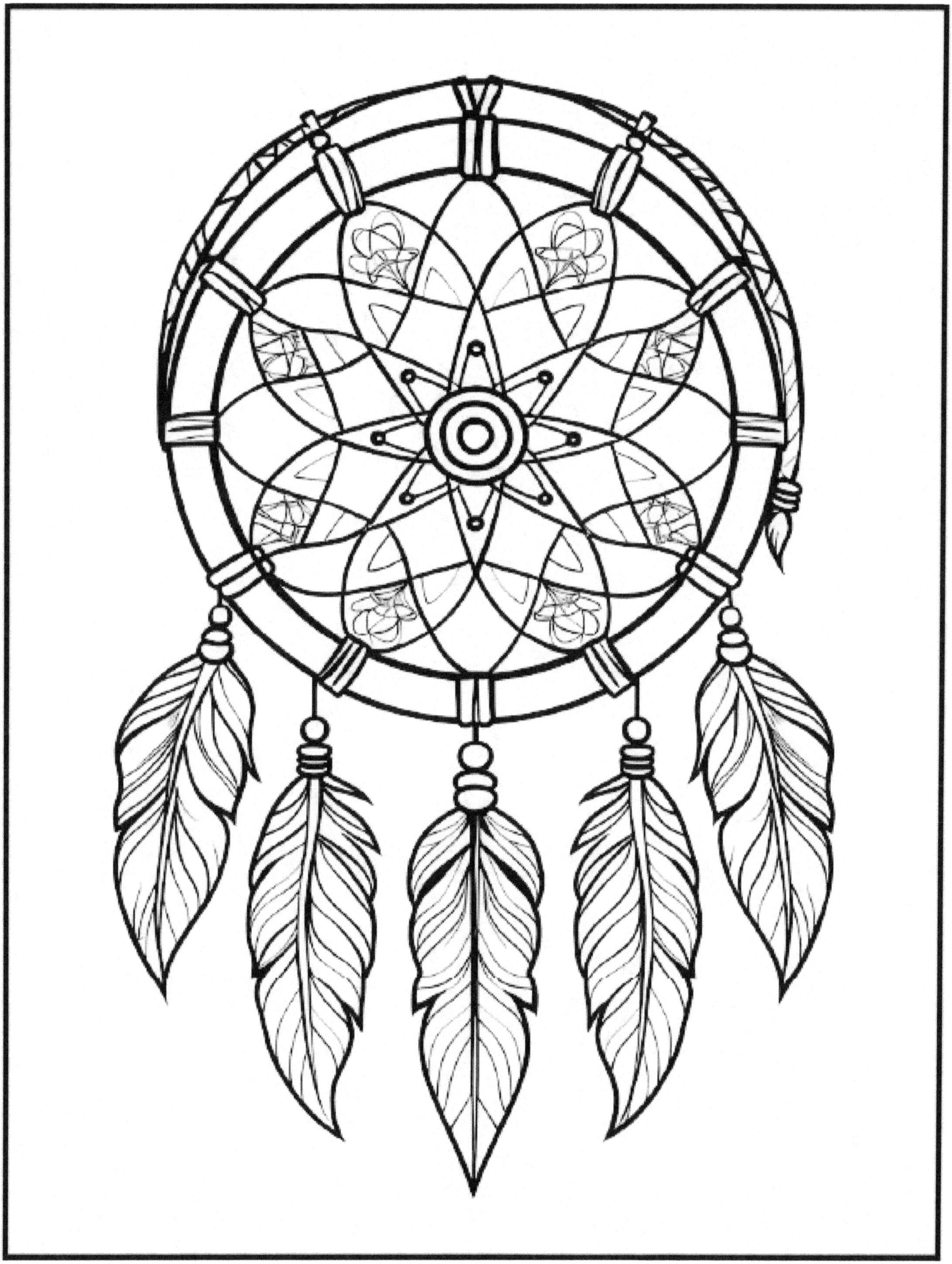

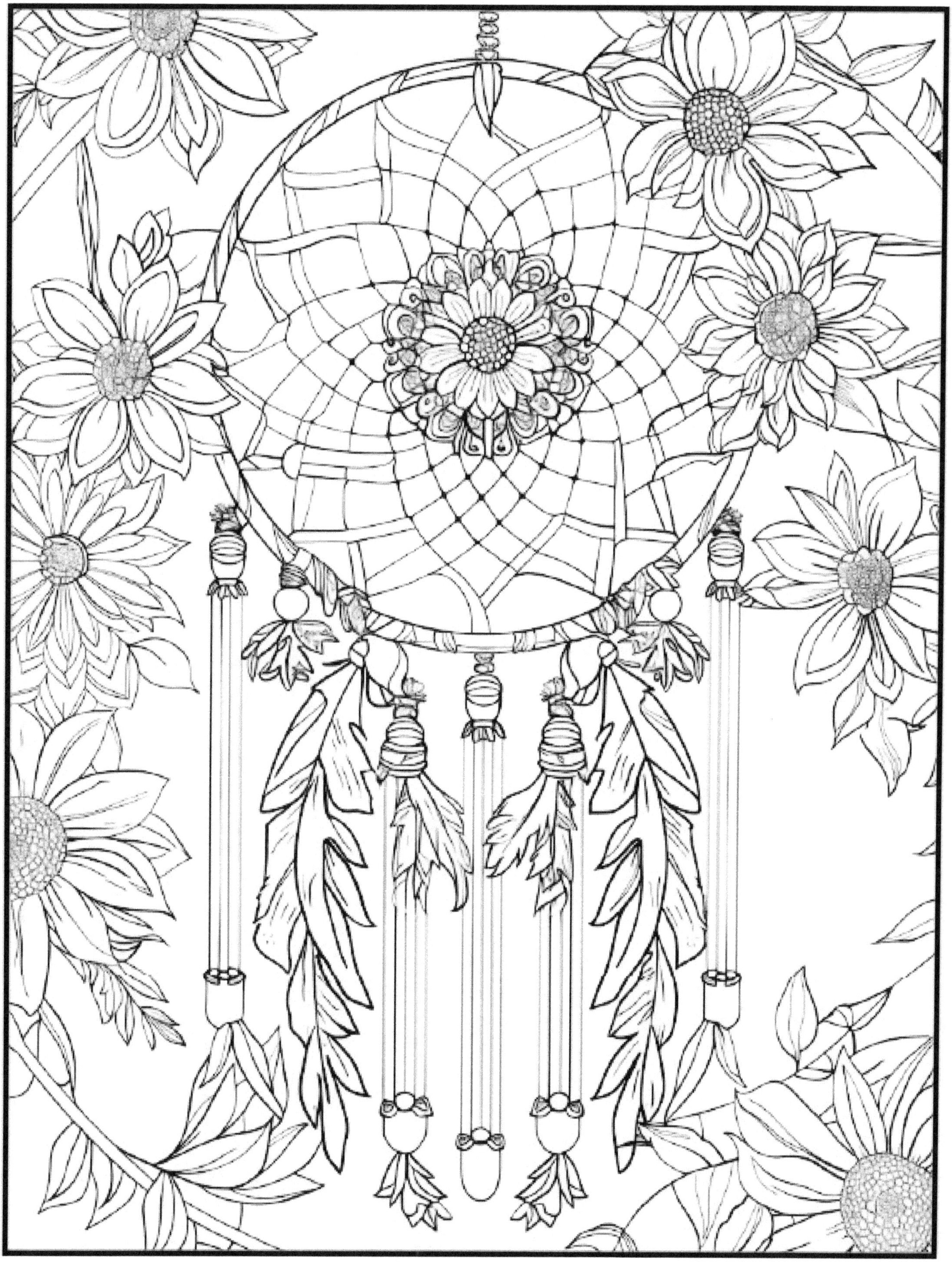

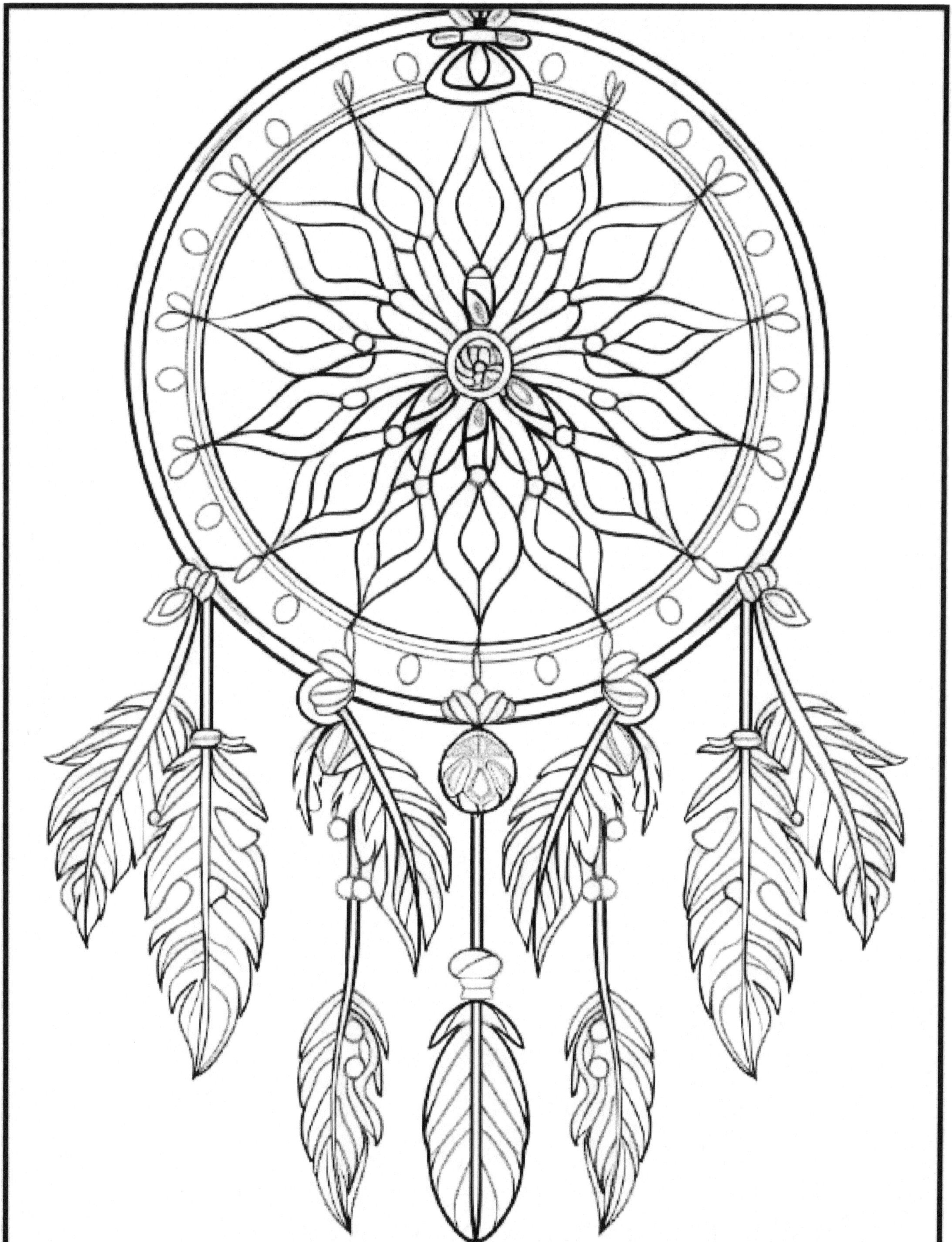

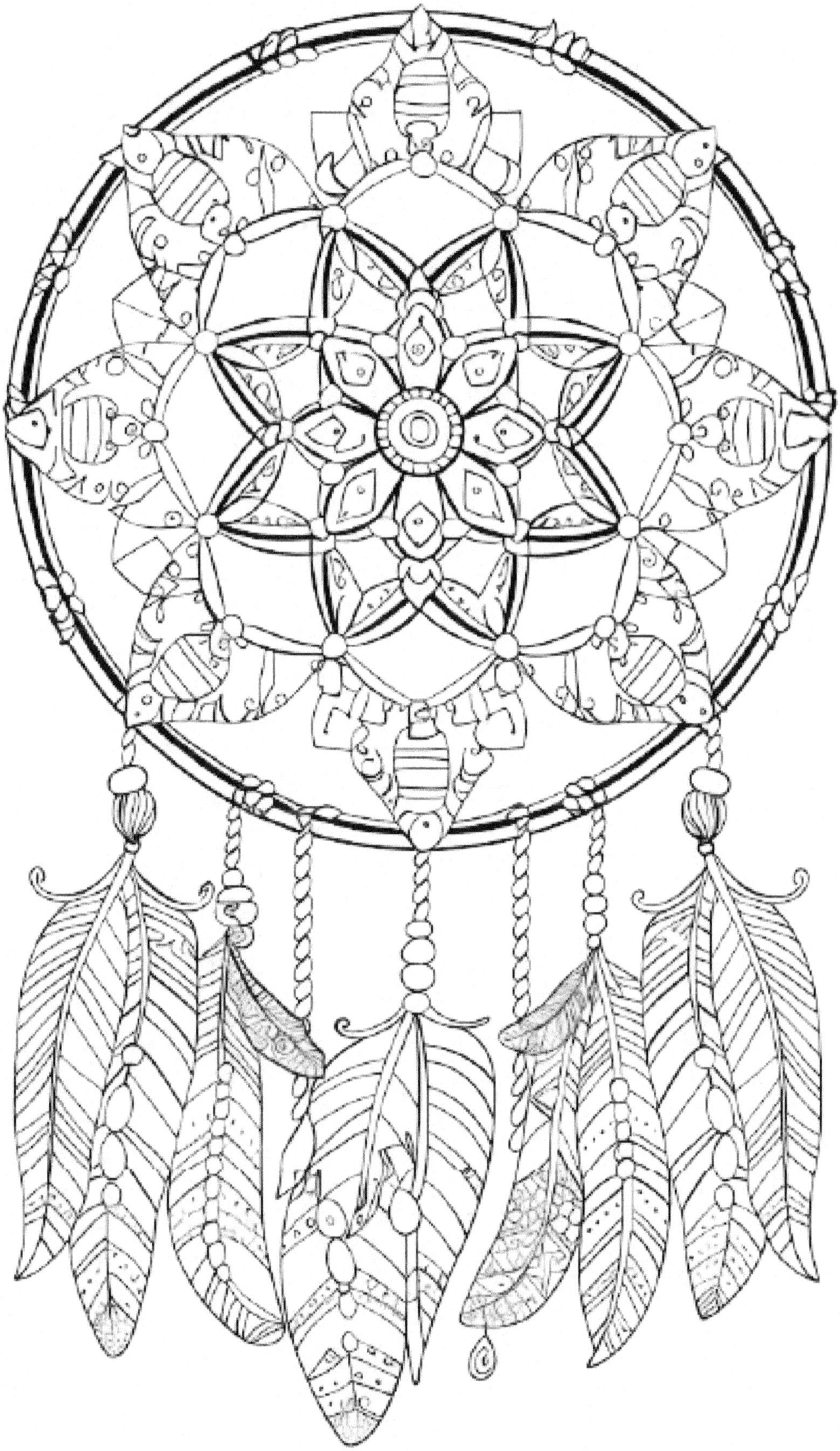

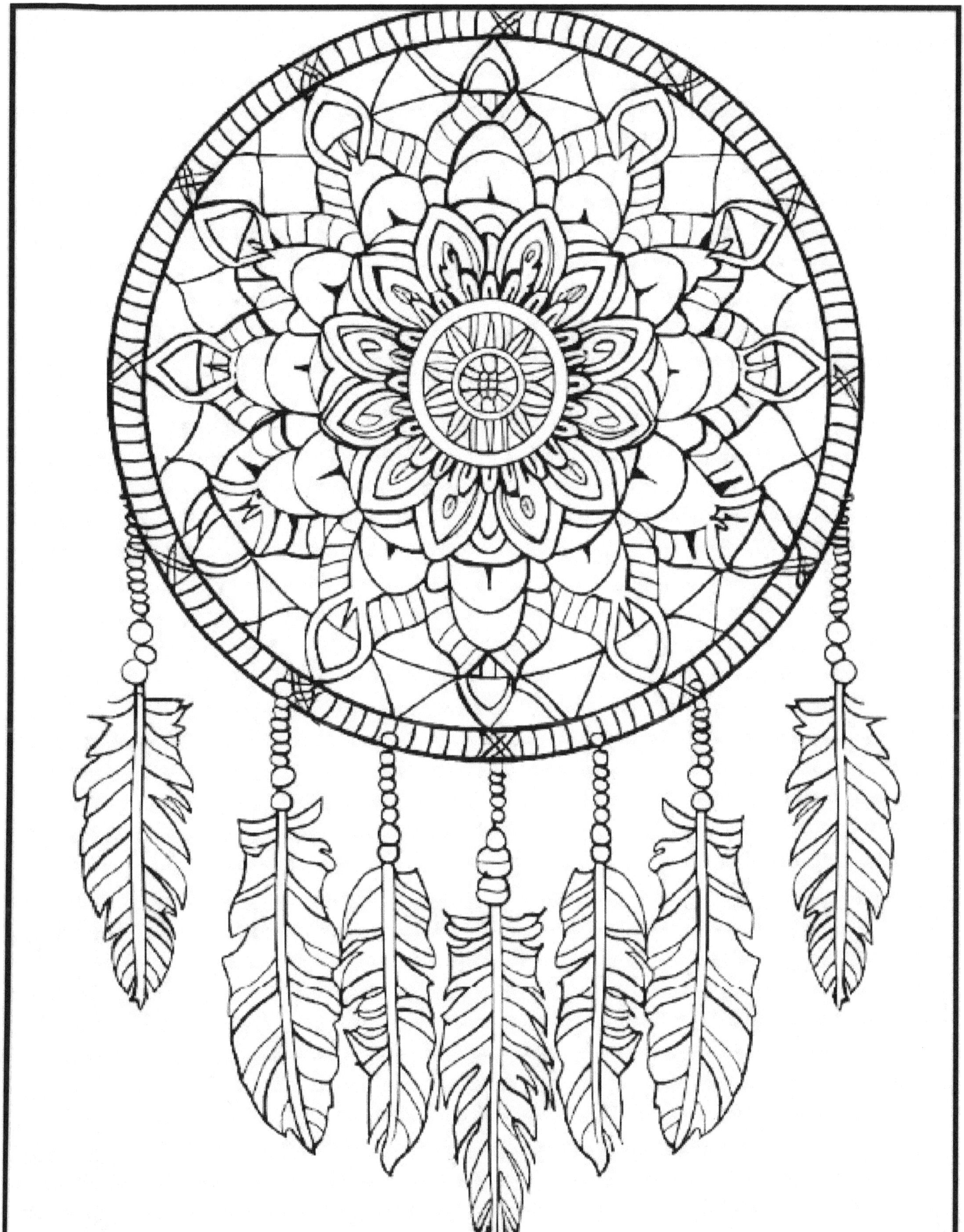

www.ingramcontent.com/pod-product-compliance
Lightning Source LLC
Chambersburg PA
CBHW082112220526
45472CB00009B/2155
* 9 7 9 8 3 2 7 8 8 1 9 4 5 *